SCHOLASTIC

CW00726454

YOU CAN

Have a GREEN SCHOOL

Anthony David

Eco-Schools

FOR AGES
4-11

"Sustainable development will not
just be a subject in the classroom; it
will be in its bricks and mortar"

Tony Blair

Acknowledgements

Author
Anthony David

Editor
Nicola Morgan

Development Editor
Kate Pedlar

Project Editor
Fabia Lewis

Series Designer
Catherine Perera

Cover Designer
Anna Oliwa

Cover photography
© Getty Images/ Jade Albert Studio, Inc.

Design
Q2a Media

Text © 2008, Anthony David
© 2008, Scholastic Ltd

Designed using Adobe InDesign

Published by Scholastic Ltd
Villiers House
Clarendon Avenue
Leamington Spa
Warwickshire CV32 5PR

www.scholastic.co.uk

Printed by Bell and Bain Ltd.
1 2 3 4 5 6 7 8 9   8 9 0 1 2 3 4 5 6 7

I would like to thank the children, families and staff of Highgate Primary School, Terrance Bengtson and Dr Nick Sireau who have all contributed in many ways to the development of this book. A.D.

Eco-Schools logo, on the front cover, reproduced with the kind permission of Eco-Schools.

British Library Cataloguing-in-Publication Data
A catalogue record for this book is available from the British Library.
ISBN 978-1407-10083-8

The right of Anthony David to be identified as the author of this work has been asserted by him in accordance with the Copyright, Designs and Patents Act 1988.

All rights reserved. This book is sold subject to the condition that it shall not, by way of trade or otherwise, be lent, hired out or otherwise circulated without the publisher's prior consent in any form of binding or cover other than that in which it is published and without a similar condition, including this condition, being imposed upon the subsequent purchaser.

No part of this publication may be reproduced, stored in a retrieval system, or transmitted, in any form or by any means, electronic, mechanical, photocopying, recording or otherwise, without the prior permission of the publisher. This book remains in copyright, although permission is granted to copy pages where indicated for classroom distribution and use only in the school which has purchased the book, or by the teacher who has purchased the book, and in accordance with the CLA licensing agreement. Photocopying permission is given only for purchasers and not for borrowers of books from any lending service.

Due to the nature of the web, the publisher cannot guarantee the content or links of any of the websites referred to. All links were checked January 2008, but It is the responsibility of the reader to assess the suitability of websites and check that links are still live.

Every effort has been made to trace copyright holders for the works reproduced in this book, and the publishers apologise for any inadvertent omissions.

Contents

Contents

Foreword from Solarcentury

Forty years ago, in school, I was fascinated by rocks and fossils. I studied geology and learned about the natural rhythms of our planet over millions of years.

Thirty years ago, I finished my studies and became a teacher. I wanted to share my love of the planet with students, and teach them what I had learned about detective work into Earth's past. When not teaching, I did more of that detective work. The more I discovered, the more I saw how fragile – how fundamentally changeable – the planet is.

Twenty years ago, scientists began to worry about the impact on the planet of burning fossil-fuels: oil, coal and gas. When we burn these fuels, greenhouse gases result. These gases trap heat in the Earth's thin atmosphere. Today, every school child learns about the climate change we risk when we burn fossil fuels. We have to stop taking these risks, and soon.

The good news is that there are many ways we can help to stop greenhouse gas emissions. Most of them have to do with the way we use energy. We can replace oil, coal and gas with renewable energy sources. We can also improve energy efficiency and energy conservation.

Ten years ago, I set up a small company to install as many solar cells and panels on buildings as possible. I didn't do this because solar is the magic solution, it is a single member of a big family of solutions; nothing more and nothing less. But it is a neat solution and I have always thought it to be a bit magical, just sitting there with no moving parts, generating either electricity (if solar photovoltaic cells are used) or hot water (if solar thermal panels are used). So, I concentrated on solar as one way for one person to show that you can do something about climate change.

Since then, Solarcentury has installed solar on more than 600 buildings. We have also installed solar on more than 50 schools. In each of those schools, many hundreds of schoolchildren will see the solar at work over the lifetime of the system, and see that there is a way to produce energy without greenhouse emissions: a way you can do things differently. As a result of this, and because the letters Solarcentury gets from schoolchildren about these installations are my favourite letters, school installations are my favourite. They are, to me, like candles for hope in our problematic world.

There are many environmental and social problems including climate change and there are many solutions. We can solve these problems. I hope this book will help many school children find out how we can, and act on it, having fun along the way.

You can!

Jeremy Leggett

Foreword from Eco-Schools

Climate change is big, really BIG; its impact is being felt all around the globe. Barely a week goes by without yet another environmental disaster being reported in the media, whether it's desertification in Africa, flooding in India or even the lack of snow in Aviemore.

While it's clear that each and every one of us has a role to play, it's also increasingly apparent that children and young people are passionate about tackling climate change and determined to make a difference.

Schools have a vital role to play in encouraging this and although climate change is touched upon in the curriculum, schools still struggle to give the topic the attention it deserves.

In the last few years, thousands of schools in England have made a commitment towards becoming more sustainable via the International Eco-Schools programme. Indeed, many of them have integrated the programme's principles into their own curriculum and have had some spectacular results.

Whether your school is looking to take its first steps towards getting your students involved or looking for ways to engage with your local community, this book is an excellent resource. It clearly sets out the issues and offers a range of fantastic and engaging ways in which you might help children make a difference.

Andrew Suter
Programmes Manager, Eco-Schools

Introduction

In the last decade, environmental sustainability has gone from being a 'nice idea' to front page headlines. Since the Kyoto Protocol was agreed on 11th December 1997, the world has woken up to the fact that not only are we experiencing extreme climate change but that oil, our primary energy source, is rapidly becoming a scarce commodity. Media speculation has reached such fever pitch that it would be difficult to open any paper and not find one, two or three lead environmental articles. Political parties are equally aligning themselves in support of environmental policies, with key parties even changing their logos to show their commitment to this growing issue.

Children's exposure to this subject has also been accelerated by the impact of the communications revolution. Not only do they know more about what is happening in the world but they learn about it in a heart beat. Whereas children were aware of acid rain destruction in the late 1970s and early 1980s, they simply did not have the access to images, information and social networks that children have today. Unsurprisingly, The Primary Review found that children, when discussing the wider world, placed environmental changes as a significant concern for their immediate future. It found that:
'The soundings programme as a whole was pervaded by a sense of deep pessimism about the future, to which children themselves were not immune. Many expressed concern about climate change, global warming and pollution, and optimists were balanced by those who felt that governments were not doing enough to respond to the urgency and magnitude of the challenges.'
(The Primary Review: *Community Soundings*, Alexander and Hargreaves)

Given this change of emphasis it is somewhat surprising that sustainability is still a new subject within schools particularly when the Review noted that:
'…where schools had started engaging children with global and local realities as aspects of their education they were noticeably more upbeat. In several schools children were involved in environmental and energy-saving projects and the sense that "we can do something about it" seemed to make all the difference.'
(The Primary Review: *Community Soundings*, Alexander and Hargreaves)

As a hub within the community, schools are best placed to make that difference. This book sets out to demonstrate how schools can support environmental sustainability, without compromising valuable curriculum time but empowering the children, parents and staff about sustainable education.

It is a whole school issue and each member can, with little change to their daily habits, make a collective contribution towards improving their environment as a whole.

You Can... Involve children

Increasingly, children are given meaningful opportunities to have a positive impact on their learning environment through consultation or school councils. Equally schools are, more than ever, looking for opportunities to give their children a voice and environmental projects can lend themselves easily to this.

Thinking points

● The Primary Review Soundings (2007) took the views and opinions from over 190 school councils and pupil groups around the country. When considering a global perspective its conclusions where that: 'Many [children] expressed concern about climate change, global warming and pollution, and optimists were balanced by those who felt that governments were not doing enough to respond to the urgency and magnitude of the challenges.'

● However, where schools were actively engaging with these global issues as part of the children's education, they found that: '...they [the children] were noticeably more upbeat. In several schools children were involved in environmental and energy-saving projects and the sense that 'we can do something about it' seemed to make all the difference. This more positive outlook was most evident in the school whose environmental activism was spearheaded by an 'Eco-action' group with representatives from each year. 'This is an indicator that pupils are ready to support schools in environmental projects and see it as important for their future.

Tips, ideas and activities

● Consider renaming your school council 'eco-school council' to give it a positive alliance towards sustainable learning.

● Write an eco-school action plan with the eco-school council.

● Create mini-teams within the council who have specific functions, such as counting the number of children who cycle to school; updating the termly energy grid with the site manager; counting Yellow Pages for the Yellow Woods Challenge (see www.yellow-woods.co.uk and page 32); forming a lunchtime litter team. This will instil a sense of unity and meaning within the mini-team while still being accountable to a larger body. Ensure that all members of staff are up to date with the eco-school council's 'to do' lists.

● Invite a governor to join your eco-school council.

● Involve your school council and key members of staff in writing environmental policies.

● Encourage each class to write an 'energy reduction' statement and to label things where appropriate (it could be as simple as 'Use our resources carefully – reduce' written on a pencil pot or 'Don't forget to turn me off' on a class computer.)

● If you are asking the children to act on a part of the eco-school action plan, ensure that it is clear what you are asking them to do and why they are doing it. For example, if you are encouraging children to walk to school, how can you support those who come by car? (You could encourage 'park and stride' initiatives where children are driven part of the way and walk the rest.)

● Below are two useful websites that could help inform, resource and develop a working eco-school council:
www.schoolcouncils.org
www.primaryreview.org.uk

You Can... **Involve families**

For a green project to work it needs the full thrust of committed professionals, enthusiastic children and caring families. Parents and carers want to support schools and will often be more than willing to be involved with environmental projects. It is an opportunity for them to show that they value their child's learning experience and want to be part of it. Once engaged, you may be surprised by how organised they are on the school's behalf.

Thinking points

● It should go without saying that parents have the greatest impact on their child's education. A child will reflect their parents' views and express their values. If you can get parents involved with green issues, the children will follow. That said, there is a lot of value in 'pester power' and if a child wants something badly enough (such as a cycling to school certificate) they can help influence a parent's decision. In this case, it is up to the school to manage these situations so that parents and children feel supported.

● You will have a broad skills base amongst your parenting community. It is highly likely that there will be keen gardeners, people involved in the Forestry Commission or Woodland Trust or those who simply have the skills to organise other parents. Use these people. It will show that the school values their skills and help you to delegate responsibilities.

Tips, ideas and activities

● When you are launching a new project, clearly state your expectations of parents. If it is a walk to school or cycling project, give suggestions in your letter as to how parents can support their children. Think about those who would not be able to take part – how can you include them? Is there another way into the project that will value these children (they may be involved with designing posters, for example?)

● Parents are great organisers. Tap into this. If they can organise 10 or 15 children to go to the park after school then it is reasonable to think that with little encouragement they can organise car pooling with friends. Your annual School Travel survey (see page 62 for a photocopiable survey) should reveal how much car pooling occurs in your school. If it is a low figure (less than 10%) it is relatively easy to increase this with a few letters or words of encouragement.

● Give incentives. If you are encouraging children to collect Yellow Pages (see page 32 or www.yellow-woods.co.uk) then award the family who collected the most by getting their photograph in the local newspaper. Your local newspaper will be very happy to support the school. Also celebrate parents who have helped the most – you may want to give out 'parent taxi' certificates to parents who car pool or 'my parent walked to school' prizes alongside children's prizes.

● Involve your parents in healthy events. It may be that a number of members of staff are taking part in a fun run or fun cycle. Invite parents to take part. As these events usually take place on Saturdays, it will give working parents an opportunity to be involved with the school.

● Below are a number of useful websites that could help support parents with environmental projects in school:
www.parentingeducationmaterials.co.uk
www.bhf.org.uk
www.primaryreview.org.uk

You Can... **Involve the staff community**

Like yourself, your colleagues will most likely share a concern about today's changing environment. It is useful to reassure colleagues that there are simple things we can do that will have a positive impact. It's not just a case of installing expensive solar panels; turning off a computer at the end of the day saves energy (and money!) and is a healthy habit to get into. What you should be aiming towards is a shared responsibility; we are all in this together.

Thinking points

● Although bicycles have gone down in price, they are still very much a luxury item. However more and more businesses and local authorities are buying into schemes that will either enable staff to buy a bicycle at a reduced price or take it out of their gross salary in 12 instalments. This makes owning a bike more attractive, even if it is for recreational purposes only. If you do not know what schemes are available, contact your local school travel advisor.

● As with any new scheme, it is best to audit your staff skills. If you have not been involved in any previous environmental projects or have limited experience this will inevitably involve some change. This change must be managed with care and concerns should be addressed from the beginning. As with any new element to the school it should be monitored and its impact evaluated appropriately.

Tips, ideas and activities

● Sustrans (www.sustrans.org.uk) offer training sessions for members of staff who wish to become cycle trainers. This is a nationally accepted certification that enables an adult to teach up to stage 3 cycle training in the UK.

● If there is a member of staff who does not know how to ride a bike, they are entitled to free training sessions and should be directed to the local school travel officer.

● Colleagues can support environmental schemes in many small ways, such as car pooling, organising litter monitors, switching off lights or computers at the end of the day and being interested in activities such as National Tree Week (www.treecouncil.org.uk). If adults are taking an active part, then children will generally follow.

● Delegate responsibilities and use your teachers' skills. If a teacher cycles to school every day, let them be the champion for sustainable travel. Let your site manager wave the flag for energy efficiency. If a colleague is a keen gardener, encourage them to run a lunch time gardening club.

● Below are a number of useful websites that could help support colleagues with environmental projects. Generally these websites not only offer useful lesson plans but also include bite-sized chunks of information, which is ideal for the busy teacher: www.e4s.org.uk www.bbc.co.uk/schools/ teachers/environment www.gogreeninitiative.org www.savenature.org

You Can... **Be green with *Every Child Matters***

Although the Every Child Matters agenda has tended to sit alongside learning, its five core outcomes lend themselves to most environmental projects. Below is list of activities that match each of the five outcomes. This is by no means comprehensive but should serve as a launch point for environmental projects.

Thinking points

● When the *Every Child Matters* outcomes were first announced in 2005 they were met with mixed reactions. Although teachers generally saw them as guiding outcomes that all children should work towards, they were not sure how they would fit into their day-to-day curriculum. The intention of *Every Child Matters* was not to be a replacement curriculum but to provide objectives to support children's wellbeing for their future. In that context, environmentalism fits in well and, within that, a school can begin to wrap a curriculum around environmental themes.

● As a rule of thumb, schools should be looking to identify the *Every Child Matters* outcomes across the school. This may be in the school vision (see page 14), action plans, curriculum and school aims. The outcomes are purposefully broad to enable schools to expose children to as many *Every Child Matters* opportunities as possible to fully prepare them for their future.

Tips, ideas and activities

● Explain that handwriting must suit its purpose. Brevity, casual lettering and inaccurate spelling are fine for personal notes and drafts, but all writing needs to be legible. The aesthetics of handwriting can be saved for 'fair copies' or for letters for others to read.

● Below are the five *Every Child Matters* outcomes, along with green issues that would be included in each of them. These areas are dealt with in more detail throughout this book.

● **Being Healthy**
  - cycling or walking to school
  - zoning out the school play space for active sports
  - choosing healthy food options
  - composting.

● **Staying Safe**
  - learning to cross the road safely
  - choosing safe routes home
  - using gardening equipment safely
  - knowing the school site and where there are areas of risk.

● **Enjoying and Achieving**
  - involving parents and the community
  - running landmark events
  - celebrating success
  - posting work on the internet.

● **Making a Positive Contribution**
  - setting energy aims
  - being part of an eco-team
  - being a playground buddy.

● **Achieving Economic Well-being**
  - accessing grants
  - monitoring energy use
  - working towards shared goals
  - recycling as a means to raise funds.

You Can... Conduct an environmental review

Conducting an environmental review is key to formulating a sound action plan. A review should help to identify strengths and areas for development. It goes without saying that each school will have different targets; however, a good rule of thumb is to address only one or two core areas at a time. This should ensure success and, particularly in the first few months of an environmental action plan, ensure that the school community buys into this vision.

Thinking points
● What areas of the review already show success? It may be an established partnership with the Woodland Trust or a policy on recycling. Developing these areas and further enhancing them will allow them to become a topic in which the children feel they are experts and will help to embed environmental sustainability as a theme within the school. Once embedded, consider addressing new areas for development, such as energy or water use. Your local authority environmental officer should be able to support you with new projects.

● Consider conducting the survey with an environmental team that includes:

- a senior school leader
- children (possibly the school council)
- a governor
- a site manager.

This will help work towards a collective responsibility for future action.

Tips, ideas and activities
● When conducting the survey, 'walk the site'. This will help you to collect evidence for action and identify where you have established good practice.

● Conduct the survey with the Site Manager. They will hold information about current practice and can be a source of advice for future action.

● Look for leaking taps, broken radiators, cracked window frames, electrical equipment that is on standby (such as data projectors). All of these will inform your action.

● Do you have a thermostat? How does it work? Different spaces will have different heating requirements and working thermostats are both energy and financially efficient.

● How aware are you of your energy cost and use? With the increase of electrical technology in schools, bills have grown. All staff and pupils share the energy use responsibility and should be made aware of it.

● What is your energy vision? If you have one it will have an impact on your annual survey as a driver towards obtaining your vision. If you do not have a vision you should try and set some energy goals. Headteachers are accountable for how the budget is spent, which should be done wisely and efficiently.

● Review your survey annually. This will not only show where future action is needed but should also identify new strengths. This review is important as it should encourage the school community to continue with its environmental action. See pages 59–61 for a photocopiable environmental review questionnaire (supplied by Eco-Schools).

● These websites could support an environmental review:
www.environmentalreview.org
www.eco-schools.org.uk

You Can... Create a plan of action

As with any strand of school development, your environmental projects need to be planned. There may be seasonal conditions to be mindful of or financial implications but careful planning will help to ensure a greater chance of success. Take into consideration who will be responsible for key actions, that the school is on-board and that you have the resources (financial, time and physical) to implement your plan. If all these elements are in place you have improved your chances of long-term environmental change.

Thinking points

● Environmental sustainability is a broad topic. Typically it includes water, energy, transport, site management, litter, recycling (waste), healthy living, biodiversity and a global perspective. Don't try and address all of them in one year. Audit what your school does already and write a plan that works to your strengths.

● When you are considering what area to focus on consider what resources you have available. You might have a proactive school travel advisor who is able to support any travel schemes you are considering. Equally there may be an area of expertise that you have personally. Start with what you feel you can resource. It is worth having a long term vision in mind with a number of environmental milestones over two or three years. By establishing a culture of environmental sustainability within the school you can go on to build on it over the coming years.

Tips, ideas and activities

● There may be reasonable links within your school improvement priorities. Look for them. Alternatively, discuss with your School Leadership Team the possibility of creating an area of sustainability as a school improvement priority.

● Write your action plan on the common school action plan grid. Alternatively, you could use the photocopiable Environmental Action Plan grid provided on page 58. Standard action plans should have the following column headings:
  ● Actions required (steps to be taken)
  ● Action by whom
  ● Action by when
  ● Funding
  ● Monitoring – how and who
  ● Notes on progress.

● A good principle for action plans is to either tie them to an aspect of your school vision (ideally the environmental aspect) or an aspect of *Every Child Matters* (being healthy, staying safe, enjoying and achieving, making a positive contribution, economic well-being) in order to present a robust document.

● Aim to evaluate your plan at least once a term and write your action on it. If somebody needs to see your file they will want to know what progress you have made.

● Keep a school subject coordinator folder. As with any aspect of school there will be a set of common papers that you will need to archive. Index areas should include:
  ● environmental policy
  ● current action plan
  ● finance (budget and grants)
  ● communication (copies of letters and emails)
  ● project briefs.

● You should aim for no more than three activities a year. Schools are busy places and that must be respected. Aim to have a common theme with these projects, such as cycling.

You Can... **Create a vision statement**

Most schools now have a shared vision statement, often with discrete links to the Every Child Matters outcomes. In the same way, schools should be considering how to introduce elements of environmental sustainability into their vision. If schools are genuinely committed to their children's future they need to consider the world they are preparing their children for, both academically and environmentally. It is a world with an uncertain future and we should be preparing our children for it at all levels.

Thinking points

● Why is a vision necessary? The vision is a slightly grand way of saying 'this is where we want to go' and for that you need vision. In short it means 'we see'. That said, a good school vision goes beyond that as it also describes the school's values and ethos. By definition, it represents what a school wants to achieve and if that achievement encompasses environmentalism it is also demonstrating that the schools sees this as central to the school, its community and the children it serves.

● Hillman and Stoll (1994) in research found that successful visions for a school:
  ○ expressed a desirable direction for the school
  ○ were well grounded in its circumstances
  ○ looked confidently to the future
  ○ were always a step ahead of the school's reality
  ○ were dynamic and defined the school's purpose.

(Source: National College for School Leadership)

Tips, ideas and activities

● Guided consultation is the secret to successful vision making. A school community will not buy into a vision if it is imposed – it must come from them. However, it is important to look at ways of narrowing down your consultation data.

● Generally a Governing Committee has responsibility for the wording of the vision. If you are intending to re-word or add to an existing element then it is best to approach that committee first.

● Consultation generally takes two forms: surveys or face-to-face meetings. By far the most effective are face-to-face meetings but these are most time-consuming, therefore a balance needs to be struck between resources and information. Equally, surveys can be quick to complete but take hours to interpret. If it is possible, encourage families to complete online surveys at school. This can be done on parent consultation nights when it is most likely that you will have the largest number of parents on site in one evening.

● Free survey sites such as Survey Monkey (www.surveymonkey.com) allow you to create bespoke surveys and will calculate all the results on your behalf.

● Don't forget to communicate your environmental changes with the community. Having done all the hard work, they will want to know what wording has been chosen that reflects the essence of the community's thoughts.

● Alternative online survey sites include:
www.zapsurvey.com
www.keysurvey.co.uk

You Can... Inform the SEF and work with the School Leadership Team

The Self Evaluation Form (SEF) is the backbone of the school. In essence it is the distillation of all that the school stands for and accomplishes. If written clearly it should identify the school's strengths and areas for improvement. Within this document there are three areas where environmental sustainability could be mentioned: Section 1 – characteristics of your school; Section 2 – the views of learners and other stakeholders; Section 4 – personal development and well-being.

Thinking points
● There are a large number of Kitemarks for schools to work towards and they are recognised at the front of the SEF. The evidence needed for one Kitemark may be similar to another, in which case it would be reasonable to work towards both. OFSTED are aware of these marks as they are recognition that your school has reached a national standard.

● Your School Leadership Team will be looking out for your welfare. Although environmental projects can be exciting, as they often involve the whole school community, do not feel criticised if your School Leadership Team asks you to hold back on some ideas. It is their duty of care on your behalf.

Tips, ideas and activities
● Choose your time to talk to the School Leadership Team wisely. They may well have an agreed timetable of tasks and, although there is generally a degree of flexibility, you may not be able to have the meeting time that you would want. Be professional. Ask how much time you have and at what time your agenda item is; make your intention clear (is it for advice or to inform?) and stick to your brief.

● Schools work in cycles. If you are considering a large-scale project for the next academic year, then aim to brief the School Leadership Team in May so that it can be considered as an area for school improvement for the next year. It is the headteacher's duty to inform the governors what the new school improvement priorities are by July.

● Prepare your action plan by September so that it is current and meaningful for the coming academic year.

● If you are asked to provide information for the SEF then provide what is asked for, not more or less. The document must be succinct as must your evidence of information.

● It is courteous to provide an end-of-year evaluation to the curriculum committee or School Leadership Team and it also shows that you are being rigorous.

● Celebrate success and credit your support.

You Can... **Set up an eco-team**

Eco-teams not only state what they are about, they also serve to give children a meaningful voice when it comes to the subject of environmental sustainability. As a result of this, children take a lot of pride in being involved in a team and it is important to celebrate this in assemblies, letters and around the school (such as having a dedicated eco-teams' display board in the heart of the school).

Thinking points

● Increasingly schools are looking at how they can give their pupils a 'voice'. This can be done effectively through school councils or student surveys. However, action teams with a sustainable mandate offer a 'real-life' opportunity where children can act for their future benefit. The Primary Review noted in its initial soundings that: 'In several schools children were involved in environmental and energy-saving projects and the sense that 'we can do something about it' seemed to make all the difference. This more positive outlook was most evident in the school whose environmental activism was spearheaded by an 'Eco-action' group with representatives from each year.'

● In these cases, it is not simply a case of giving children some responsibility, it is about positively allowing them to take control of their future and giving them the tools so that they 'can do something about it'.

Tips, ideas and activities

● Teams do not need to be large and they are a useful way of mixing year groups. Below is a breakdown of how a typical primary could use school council members (or two representatives from each class) in a range of eco-teams:

  ● Years 1 and 2 – Litter and Recycling Team responsible for: Yellow Pages collection (see www.yellow-woods.co.uk or page 32); composting of fruit and vegetables from the kitchen or classes; and highlighting the importance of where to place your litter.

  ● Years 3 and 4 – Energy Team responsible for: calculating the school's termly spend on energy and water; identifying how the school can improve on its energy use; and having a good working relationship with the site manager.

  ● Years 5 and 6 – Travel Team: responsible for leading 'walk to school' campaigns; for keeping a regular record of how many people (adults and children) cycle to school; and leading 'park and stride' campaigns for those families for whom driving is a necessity (children are driven part of the way and walk the rest.)

Feedback from these teams can then form part of the school council agenda.

● Celebrate news and success on a display board in the heart of the school. Yellow Pages collections, bike tallies and energy updates help to keep displays alive and a relevant talking point.

● Support teams by inviting outside experts to work alongside them to advise their action. These people could be the local authority sustainability officer, wardens from a local wood, environmental officers or school travel advisers.

● Below are a number of useful websites that could help inform, resource and develop a working eco-team:
www.schoolsgarden.org.uk
www.schoolcouncils.org
www.teachers.gov.uk/growingschools
www.primaryreview.org.uk

You Can... Go green in an urban environment

Increasingly, the urban environment is becoming the new habitat for wildlife and with little modification schools can present a meaningful sustainable environment that complements and supports local wildlife. Even if your school is surrounded by 'the concrete jungle' there are still plenty of energy reductions, recycling projects, water reductions, litter initiatives and transport schemes you can be involved with that have a real impact on school life. Projects such as Yellow Woods (see p32) and WOW (Walk Once a Week – www.walktoschool.org.uk) have their greatest impact in high-density areas.

Thinking points

● Arguably urban schools are in a better position to act positively on environmental projects than rural schools simply because currently more money is being directed towards them.

● It is important to consider and understand your site and what can be achieved. What is your aim when starting an environmental project? In all cases, there is nothing to lose by aiming high.

● One school, after carrying out an audit, discovered that only 22% of its children walked to school yet over 80% of them lived within a reasonable walking distance. This school decided to run a walking project and within a year over 75% of the children were walking to school at least once a week. This was a great delight to the school but given the data it knew it was possible.

Tips, ideas and activities

● Have you conducted an environmental audit? If not how could you involve the children, staff or local families? At the back of this book is an audit (see pages 59–61) that you could use to start developing an environmental action plan. It is important to regularly review any action plan as it will not only direct future action but help celebrate success.

● Does your local authority have an environmental officer? If so, they may well be able to support the school, which could shape an environmental action plan.

● Are you aware of nationwide initiatives such as Eco-Schools, Sustainable Schools, Solar4School, and Yellow Woods? Many of the current major projects are detailed within this book and website addresses are provided on page 18.

● If you are new to sustainable learning then start with one project, such as paper recycling and build up from there. For a school to have a positive environmental impact, it does not have to have a wind turbine or solar panels on its roof. The smallest project, done correctly, can have a huge impact.

● Survey parents: they may be willing to support the school in developing micro-allotments, gardening projects or encouraging children to take part in walk to school schemes. Equally they may have a really good idea that will make you stand out from the rest and make them feel included.

● Below are some useful websites that could help inform, resource and develop an environmental action plan within an urban environment:
www.carbontrust.co.uk/energy
www.suschool.org.uk
www.teachernet.gov.uk/sustainableschools

You Can... Go green in a rural environment

It would be easy to assume that because of their setting rural schools are naturally more environmentally aware than their urban partners. While it may be true that some rural schools have well-established environmental action plans, there will still be the same challenges that all schools face, such as reducing energy consumption, having a meaningful water policy, auditing current practice and trying to keep to the idea of reduce, reuse, recycle.

Thinking points

● If your school already has well-established environmental projects that support the curriculum and sustainable learning, conduct a thorough audit – it may be a case of making some small 'tweaks' to current practice or it may reveal a whole area (such as energy reduction) that had not been previously considered.

● Consider how you can best utilise adult support from the wider community such as game wardens, farmers, forestry commission officers and other similar professionals. These are unique to the rural setting and should be used to enhance children's learning experiences.

Tips, ideas and activities

● Identify any possible rural links. These could include local farmers, the Woodland Trust, the Forestry Commission or environmental centres that are, by nature, often located rurally.

● Small schools (those with fewer than 100 pupils) may have to consider sharing resources. In these cases, try to identify environmental projects that can be replicated across schools.

● Share training with other schools. This will ensure that the same message is being spread across a wider community.

● Your staff may be stretched covering the day-to-day tasks, so consider training a parent to champion the subject. Naturally, they will need guidance but could be a useful asset particularly when procuring resources or conducting surveys.

● Does your local authority have an environmental officer? If so, they may well be able to support the school, which could shape an environmental action plan.

● Are you aware of nationwide initiatives such as Eco-Schools, Sustainable Schools, Solar4School, and Yellow Woods? Many of the current major projects are detailed within this book and their websites are listed below. They may be able to offer specific support to your school.

● If you are new to sustainable learning then start with one project, such as paper recycling and build up from there. For a school to have a positive environmental impact it does not have to have a wind turbine or solar panels on its roof. The smallest project, done correctly, can have a huge impact.

● These websites could help inform, resource and develop an environmental action plan within a rural environment:
www.eco-schools.org.uk
www.solar4schools.co.uk
www.yellow-woods.co.uk

You Can... Use books, documentaries and films to support children

You would be hard-pressed to open a newspaper and not find an environmental article. More often than not it would be a major headline, such is the urgency of feeling towards this topic. Five years ago that would not have been the case but a number of significant books and films have helped to turn that around and bring scientific discussions into living rooms and schools.

Thinking points

● As with any new subject it is important to have a firm grounding in what you are teaching. Try to learn at least some key facts and theories but do not worry if you do not know it all. As with all primary lessons there will be some subjects where you feel you have a reasonable authority and others where you are literally one step ahead of the class. Ultimately you are aiming to teach children how they can do their bit for the environment. One step ahead is better than no steps at all.

● Documentaries and books have become more accessible and are increasingly the themes for blockbuster films and television programmes. In the latter case it is important to differentiate between science fiction and scientific evidence. That said, documentaries such as Leonardo DiCarprio's *11th Hour* or Al Gore's *An Inconvenient Truth* are easily digestible, clear and, most importantly, short.

Tips, ideas and activities

● **Books**
  ◦ *Half Gone* (Portobello Books, 2005) and *The Carbon War* (Penguin 1999) both by Jeremy Leggett give a rich history relating to how we have reached the carbon consumption of today. A former 'Oil Finder' who had a change of heart, Jeremy now runs a successful solar energy company and has launched two solar charities: Solar4Schools and Solar Aid.

● **Films**
  ◦ *An Inconvenient Truth* (Paramount Home Entertainment, 2006) is, in its simplest form, a PowerPoint® lecture by an ex-presidential hopeful. However, once watched you will be hard-pushed not to reach the conclusion that the time is now and we must act.

● **TV series**
  ◦ *Earth: The Power of the Planet* (BBC, 2007) is a stunning five-part documentary written and presented by Dr Iain Stewart. Both he and his co-writer, John Lynch, have a skill in taking complicated science and turning it into something that is entertaining and easy to understand.
  ◦ *Wild Weather* (BBC, 2002) is a four-part documentary presented by Donal MaCintyre who manages the trick of turning weather into an adrenalin sport. Ahead of its time, this series is one that children love – particularly the *Wet* episode!

● **Websites**
  ◦ www.changingthepresent.org
  ◦ www.who.int/globalchange
  ◦ www.solar4schools.co.uk

You Can... **Set energy aims**

An average a primary school budgets for around £25,000 to cover all energy costs. Over the next few years, this figure will increase well above inflation as the price of fuel continues to rise. In all likelihood this is the most expensive school bill, yet we tend to do little about it: windows are left open in winter; doors aren't closed; computers are left on over the holidays. We're not all guilty but a set of shared energy aims can at least act as a reminder for all.

Thinking points
● A computer and monitor left on over the weekend costs around £45 per year. If a whole ICT suite is left on that can be as much as £1500. It doesn't take long to do the maths and realise how much is wasted by not turning machines off at night. By keeping them on standby they still use between 70–90% of their total energy consumption. If it is possible, configure computers to default to a 'shut down' mode rather than 'log-off'. This will ensure the machine is off at night.

● Increasingly, schools are buying into wind turbines and solar panelling. Effectively they are decentralising their energy use form the national grid. Although this will off-set some energy costs it is only fair to be honest with children as to their total effectiveness, which may be limited. As a school you have a responsibility to educate children about the potential of this technology.

Tips, ideas and activities
● Ask children to identify where we use energy in the school. What do we mean by energy? Do they understand the difference between using gas or electricity?

● Through your school council distil a set of energy aims that could include:
  ◦ Turn off the interactive whiteboard or data projector when it's not being used.
  ◦ Switch off computers at the end of the day.
  ◦ Turn off lights in the summer or on sunny days.
  ◦ Turn off taps.
  ◦ Turn down radiators: do we really need all of them on?
  ◦ Turn off fans when we are not in the classroom.

● Children create a lot of body heat. Ask yourself if you need all of your heaters on, particularly in those months when the weather is changing. General advice is that rooms should be around 17°C. Children and colleagues should not be cold but neither should they be hot.

● There are a number of new building programmes for schools. If you haven't got double glazing in all your rooms and modern fire safe doors, get them – it will save hundreds on your energy bills.

● Energy aims will need to be reviewed. Your site manager should have a breakdown of the energy used in previous years, which older children can compare with the most recent units used. If energy aims are being followed, there should be a reduction in the amount used. As prices increase this will not necessarily mean a drop in your bills but it might at least prevent the costs becoming too high.

● As with any householder, you have the choice to change energy supplier. If you think you are being charged too much, check the market for a better deal.

You Can... **Be energy efficient with light**

Light is wonderful! There are few moments that are more inspiring than bright sunlight after a storm or a bright sunny day. We can make more of this free resource. Electric light obscures daylight and although electric lights are necessary in the darker months, at other times of the year their use should be carefully monitored.

Thinking points

● Over the last ten years data projectors have been placed in most primary classrooms within the UK to support the use of interactive whiteboards. A projector's power (the amount of light it can omit) is measured in lumens. Typically, older projectors had fewer lumens and therefore less power. Many classes, as a consequence, have been fitted with blinds to enhance the projector's image. When the projector is used, the blinds come down and the lights go on. This is not an ideal learning environment and teachers must ensure that once the projector has been used it is turned off and the blinds are opened.

● Sunlight has a positive effect on people. Studies have shown that adults feel more relaxed, upbeat and happy when they receive direct sunlight. Children are the same. Making good use of daylight in classrooms can also reduce lighting costs by 19% (source: Carbon Trust.)

Tips, ideas and activities

● Establish a light policy. In the darker months you will use more lights but review their use during other times of the year.

● Involve your whole staff, including cleaning staff who may well turn on hall lights when they start early in the morning. Promote the habit of turning off lights.

● Light sensors are readily available. There are two types:
  - Movement sensors detect movement in the classroom. The advantage of this system is that they will automatically turn classroom lights off when they are not in use. However, you can also find yourself being plunged into darkness while children are quietly taking tests as a result of a lack of physical movement.
  - Light sensors measure the amount of lumens (the calculation used to measure light) in the room and lights are turned on or off depending on the amount of light they sense.

● Ensure that sensors are correctly placed. Movement sensors should be able to detect movement and should be pointing into the classroom; light sensors need to detect light so should not be placed in a shaded area.

● Have your windows cleaned both inside and out. If this has not been done for a while it can have a dramatic improvement on the amount of light drawn into the class. Equally, clean the glass on internal windows and doors.

● In the warmer months, open your windows. Even the clearest glass is not the same as direct natural light.

● Be mindful of using solar reflective film on your windows. Although this is an economical way of reducing the 'heating' effect of sunlight it is also the equivalent of, as one child said, putting sunglasses on your windows!

● Evaluate where you can place energy-efficient bulbs. They are competitively priced, reliant and long-lasting.

You Can... **Explore solar energy**

Solar energy is an exciting energy form. If you already have solar panels on your school or are considering them you will, most likely, have your children's unequivocal support. Solar panels, along with wind turbines, show a genuine and financial commitment by the school for environmental sustainability. Even if you can only afford one panel (and bear in mind that 'green' energy match-funding grants are available) it will demonstrate what energy possibilities are available to your children and their families.

Thinking points

● There are, essentially, two different types of solar cell: photovoltaic and thermal. Photovoltaic, as the word implies (photo = light, voltaic = electricity), converts sunlight directly into electricity. These cells are commonly referred to as PV solar cells. Once used almost exclusively in space, photovoltaic cells are used more and more in domestic situations, such as providing power for your school or home. Thermal cells are heat extractors and are useful for heating.

● Solar cells are not cheap. Your headteacher and chair of governors will have to be convinced that buying into solar energy is of good educational and financial sense. Solar cells are also heavy. A standard array can weigh as much as a small car. You will need a structural survey to ensure that your roofs are strong enough.

Tips, ideas and activities

● Solar panels are found in a wide range of devices aside from large-scale energy or heat collectors. Calculators have run off solar panels for many years and there is an increasing range of products available from small fans of cells that will charge a mobile phone or mp3 player to A4 size cells that will charge a laptop. These products are not cheap but neither are they prohibitively expensive and even one example should be considered a good investment.

● In some cases, solar cells bought for schools will come with a meter that the children can read. It is a useful data handling exercise to record the meter readings over a period of time. This is real-life data where identified trends have a real consequence and meaning.

● Involve your children in the whole scheme from when you meet with engineers and architects to the final installation. It may well be a unique opportunity for them.

● Schools in Andalusia, Spain, routinely have solar panels installed across all available roof space and a few UK boroughs and counties are considering following the same route. Panels are very efficient – they require daylight in most cases not just pure sunlight.

● Think big. Even if you can only afford one panel at a time it is worth evaluating your total roof space. Decentralised energy collection is far more efficient than that found in your standard plug socket. Effectively you need to collect less than you do when relying on centralised mains electricity.

You Can... **Use wind turbines**

Renewable energy sources, such as wind turbines, are relatively new energy options for schools. The first Scottish primary school to install a turbine, Collydean Primary School in Glenrothes, Fife, only did so in spring 2004. However, even given this short trial period and as part of the 10-year Children's Plan, Ed Balls, England's Schools Secretary, announced at the end of 2007 that the government would be committing over £200 million to installing greener technologies into schools, which include wind turbines along with biomass fuel boilers and solar technology.

Thinking points

● Does you location have a regular wind supply? Do you have a site that is elevated more than 10 metres? If not, then it would be worth seeking advice before installing a wind turbine. Unlike solar panels it is very obvious when a wind turbine is not working and many urban areas are not suited to using one.

● Both main political parties have made it clear that public buildings such as schools should be in a position to produce their own green energy by 2016 as part of reducing the size of their carbon footprint and working towards a carbon-neutral goal.

Tips, ideas and activities

● The advantages of wind turbines are:
  ● Wind power enables electricity to be produced in an environmentally friendly way – the turbines don't produce chemical or radioactive emissions.
  ● The ground on which the turbines are positioned can still be used for agricultural purposes – such as grazing sheep.
  ● If the turbines need to be dismantled, there is no damage to the environment and no residues are left behind.

● Off-shore wind farms are expected to provide the energy needs for nearly all homes in the UK by 2020. Invite a local energy provider to the school to explain how they work and how they can help reduce the community's carbon footprint.

● Visit a local wind farm. Most farmers and some stores (such as Tesco) have large turbines or mini-wind farms on their sites.

● Invite your local MP to the school to discuss how they will support the school in reducing its carbon footprint. Alternatively, children can write to them. Your MP will write back to each child and should forward their questions and thoughts to the appropriate governmental department who will also reply to the children.

● Keep an eye out for grants – they are increasingly common and can often be used to match-fund larger projects.

● If you do install wind turbines, aim to include an energy read-out that the children can easily view. This will encourage them to calculate and record how much energy the turbine is producing and, ultimately, how much the school is saving.

● Below are a number of useful websites that could help inform, resource and develop wind turbines at your school:
www.energysavingtrust.org.uk
www.bwea.com/small/cases.html
www.carbontrust.co.uk

You Can... **Save a flush!**

Two devices, the Water Hippo and Save-a-Flush, have been available for a number of years and are straightforward to install in cisterns. The Water Hippo works by filling up with water and reducing the amount of available water space within the cistern. The Save-a-Flush performs in the same way but in this case a porous bag is filled with beads that swell when they come into contact with water. Both devices, once installed, can have a dramatic effect on your school's water consumption.

Thinking points

● How many toilets do you have in the school? The average toilet saves 45 gallons a year with one Water Hippo or Save-a-Flush. Question the children on how much water they would save if they installed such devices.

● At the Centre for Alternative Technology (CAT) in Wales, they have pioneered a range of toilet devices including waterless toilets, reed recycling systems and toilets that rely purely on rain water. This last example relies on an established system of water that, although not possible in many schools, could at least be investigated and discussed. A useful debate could be that water used for flushing does not have to be as pure as drinking water. Indeed, making it this clean is a poor use of funds - how could a school store and circulate water collected from rainfall and is this a possible way forward?

Tips, ideas and activities

● Water Hippos or Save-a-Flush packets can be sourced from either your local authority or your local water service provider. In most cases they are free and, increasingly, water service providers will also send enough for a school to give to each family if asked.

● If you are unable to source devices such as Water Hippos then either an upturned brick or a small, filled, plastic bottle will have the same effect once carefully placed in the cistern.

● Involve your site manager with your children when installing devices – it will value her/his contribution and enable the children to work with a different adult in the school.

● Survey the stopcocks and toilet area taps. Any defaults should be replaced and although this is a short-term cost, it will have a positive impact on your water bill.

● Use this activity as an opportunity to reinforce hygiene, such as hand washing and toilet flushing. Remind children to properly dry their hands and to dispose of paper towels properly.

● Audit how often urinals flush. There will be peak periods (such as break times) when they will need to be flushed more often but during the general school day this will not be the case. Sensors can be placed onto urinals to flush automatically after use, rather than periodically throughout the whole day. Urinal flush control is not expensive and could contribute to wider savings in water costs.

● Below are a number of useful websites that could help source or suggest how to use water saving devices:
www.save-a-flush.co.uk
www.hippo-the-watersaver.co.uk
www.teachernet.gov.uk/sustainableschools
www.eco-schools.org.uk

You Can... **Develop a water policy**

Water is not free. Increasingly water bills are becoming as expensive as fuel bills. This is not because of a lack of it (our particular geographic position ensures that the UK enjoys a wetter than average climate) but is due to the rising costs in treating water, which are being passed on to the user. That said there is enough evidence, both anecdotal and academic, that shows children who are properly hydrated work better. It is a case of being smart with the water we have and working towards a policy that reflects good water management.

Thinking points

● Although 70% of the world is covered in water, less than 3% is drinking water. Given that two thirds of that drinking water is locked up in glaciers and ice sheets and that most is found underground, only 0.3% is actually available on land. Most of that water is located at just two sites: Lake Baikal, Russia and the Great Lakes of America. The remaining 0.05% of freshwater is distributed around the rest of the world. Water is, in every sense, a precious commodity.

● Approximately 1/5 of the world does not have access to affordable fresh water and just under half the world does not have access to adequate sanitation. Often this is due to the cost of purifying the existing water. Without water a human will die in three days.

Tips, ideas and activities

● A water policy should cover two main themes: site management of water and drinking water opportunities.

● As a general guide, the site manager should regularly check all taps and piping at least once a year. A leaking tap or water fountain can lose litres of water a day if unchecked. Any discovered leaking tap, pipe or fountain should be fixed at the earliest opportunity.

● Install a water meter. This will allow the students and site manager to monitor the water use.

● Install water saving devices such as 'Save-a-Flush' or Water Hippos (see page 24) to maximise the water efficiency of toilets.

● Review the opportunities for access to drinking water both for children and staff. Water fountains are relatively inexpensive to install. Consider placing a water fountain inside – this will encourage children to have a drink when it is either cold or wet outside where most fountains are generally located.

● Site a fountain in the staffroom as hydrated staff will generally perform better. Coffee will dehydrate the body as well as stimulate it with caffeine.

● Encourage children to bring a water bottle into the class. This will require some training and it is worth informing parents that water bottles need daily washing, will need to be filled with fresh water each morning and that their child's name should be written on it using an indelible pen.

● Water in classrooms is generally not suitable for drinking unless stated above the taps. This water is usually stored in central water tanks located in the school roof for use in toilets, heating and cleaning. It has not been treated for drinking purposes.

You Can... **Harvest water**

It wasn't that long ago when water butts were a standard at the bottom of any drainpipe. Today it's not necessarily the case but water butts are relatively quick to install and the water they collect is more than worth the time taken to install them. If your school is fortunate enough to have an allotment or if you are in the position of considering micro-allotments then the nutrient-rich water collected in a water butt will be both a growth boost and welcome relief during hosepipe bans.

Thinking points

● Water harvesting is becoming increasingly common around the world, particularly in India, and some of the drier areas of USA and the UK. Water harvesters are essentially 21st century water butts and are usually placed underground. Their collection methods are very similar to butts, however their capacity is far greater and they are often supplied with an electric pump to draw out the harvested water. With this set-up harvesters are able to replace the water required for waste products, such as toilets and sinks, where the water does not need to be purified for consumption. Harvesters do require professional installation but in the long term a school can make reasonable financial saving as well as having a useful reserve of water for use around the site.

Tips, ideas and activities

● A general guide to roof space is that 1mm of water rainfall per square metre yields one litre.

● Water butts are available from most local garden centres. It would be worth considering how to develop a partnership with them as they may be willing to offer some support such as matching one purchased water butt for another or a price reduction. At the very least they would be able to offer valuable advice on where to place them in order to maximise your yield.

● Locating a water butt is important and whoever is involved in placing it should consider:
  ● Is it near the location where the water will be used (such as an allotment or garden)?
  ● Is it out of the way of any passing children – the water is not for consumption and should be kept sealed.
  ● How much water does the drainpipe collect? – If it is too little then the butt will not fill and may prove to be of little use but if it is too much then it may be at risk of over-filling, in which case is there adequate drainage?

● A website search of water harvester retailers will give a range of results from across the world. If you include your postcode within the search it should narrow the field to local or national retailers.

● Companies who are advertising nationwide services will give free quotes. They will tell you if it is possible to place a harvester in your school, where it should be placed and how much it would cost (at the time of print a typical commercial harvester would cost approximately £3000.)

● Below are a number of useful websites that could help inform, resource and develop water harvesting in your school:
www.wateraid.org/uk
www.water-tanks.net
www.teachernet.gov.uk/sustainableschools/framework/
framework_detail.cfm?id=37

You Can... **Compost**

Compost bins, barrels or wormeries are easily available and, in most local authorities, your environmental officer should be able to get you one for free. Compost material is a porous and highly absorbent product that is nutrient rich. Below is a list of items that you can compost. It is a useful way of involving your kitchen staff in the process of making your school sustainable by encouraging them to compost. Equally, children should be encouraged to compost their fruit peel and cores.

Thinking points

● Carefully consider where you are going to place your composter. Ideally it should be as near to the plants it is going to support as possible and placed on soil (avoid placing it on cement or tarmac as the contents will rot rather compost). Composting usually takes three months from start to finish.

● There are two basic types of composter: box heaps or wormeries. Compost heaps come in many forms but are usually either large boxes or barrel-shaped rotation composters. The difference between the two is that compostable waste is heaped into the box whereas a rotating composter rotates each time a section is filled. A wormery, as the name suggests, involves worms. A typical 'wormery' is barrel-shaped with legs and produces a significant amount of liquid fertiliser that can be tapped off. This liquid is extremely rich in nutrients and should be diluted before you use it.

Tips, ideas and activities

● Involve your kitchen staff with your 'composting team'. Kitchens create a reasonable amount of good compost material such as eggshells and vegetable peelings.

● Some tips for good composting are below:
  ● Don't throw away your kitchen scraps – add them to the compost pile. Kitchen scraps are high in nitrogen, which helps heat up the compost pile and speed up the composting process. Eggshells, coffee grounds, fruit and vegetable peels are all outstanding materials to add.
  ● If you're composting with a compost pile, bigger is often better. Heat builds up within a big pile. However, you don't want to go much bigger than about one metre by one metre.
  ● Keep your compost aerated! If you are composting with a tumbling composter, make sure you turn it whenever you add new materials. If you are composting with a pile, or in a static (non-tumbling) compost bin, be sure to mix up the contents so that the pile gets oxygen and can break down effectively.
  ● Don't let the compost completely dry out. A compost pile needs moisture to keep the composting process active.
  ● Don't keep your compost too wet so that it gets soggy and starts to stink. Just as too dry is bad, too wet is also something that you should avoid.
  ● Never put meat or cooked products into a composter as this will attract vermin.

● Below are a number of useful websites that could help source, or suggest how to use, a composter:
www.compostguide.com
www.reducerubbish.govt.nz/compost/tips.html
www.composters.com
www.wormcity.co.uk

You Can... **Have litter teams**

A number of high-profile projects such as the London Environmental Award and Eco-Schools have a significant emphasis on litter. General playground litter is usually minimal and a good litter team can raise the profile of keeping a school clean and what should be recycled or reused. A litter team can consist of school council members, or two children from each class, or a team of older children. Whatever model you choose, these children should be made fully aware that litter is not simply a crisp packet on the ground but a wider responsibility that covers the whole school.

Thinking points

● Children should always wear disposable gloves (such as medical gloves) when collecting litter. Consider how and where they can access these gloves quickly so that they avoid wasting both their own and adults' time.

● Ask the children to identify where they think litter is found around the school. Encourage them to consider areas such as the dining hall – the food dropped on the floor from either packed lunches or school dinners could be considered litter. How can this be reduced?

● Litter can be profitable (as discussed later in this book). How can your teams support collection projects such as mobile phone, battery or Yellow Pages collections? The children may have good suggestions on how the money can be spent once collected so consider how you are going to provide a forum to elicit these ideas from them.

Tips, ideas and activities

● Give each class that is involved with the free fruit for schools scheme a compost collection bin for collecting discarded fruit and vegetable pieces. Any sealable plastic container will work well but your environmental officer might be able to provide your school with bona fide compost collection bins. Once a week, two children from each class could empty the bin onto the compost heap. Empty the bins more regularly in the warmer months to avoid attracting fruit flies.

● Provide the litter team with a display area so they can advertise upcoming news or projects. Celebrate litter projects in assemblies or in letters home. If there has been a significant focus on a project (for example, a drive on collecting old ink cartridges) you may want to contact your local newspaper. Newspapers are always keen to support schools particularly when the whole-school community has been involved.

● The litter team can work with the site manager to place a 'compost litter' bin in the school grounds for children who have a compostable snack (such as an apple). It will need to be clearly labelled as it may attract other forms of litter. Once established, it will form an additional source of compost material.

● Use your team to raise the profile of litter in the dining hall. How can they tackle it? Who should be targeted?

● Aim to have a clear focus for the year. It may be reducing the amount of litter in the dining hall or playground, or it may be a home collection such as mobile phones.

● Write to parents to explain what the litter team does.

● Find information about The London Schools Environment Award and DCFS Sustainable Schools guidelines at:
www.london.gov.uk/mayor/education/lsea
www.teachernet.gov.uk/sustainableschools/framework

You Can... **Be creative with rubbish**

Rubbish can be fun. There are few times in your life when you can legitimately be totally involved with rubbish and get away with it! Be it art, poetry or a rap, children will enjoy using rubbish. And a good rap can become a theme song, which further reinforces the recycling and rubbish responsibility message.

Thinking points

● Rubbish is the solid material we throw away. The more we can recycle, the less rubbish there is. At the moment it is relatively easy to recycle paper, ink cartridges, clothes, metal and phones. Plastics are more challenging, yet the vast majority of rubbish comes from this material. Always recycle batteries or mobile phones; they produce toxic materials if left to decay.

● The amount of rubbish that the UK creates leads to some incredible figures: 3 trillion plastic bags each year; 5% of the world's population creates nearly 80% of the world's rubbish; nappies take 100 years to decompose (an average baby will use just under 2000 nappies a year); even in space there are hundreds of pieces of rubbish floating around the earth – so much so that it is becoming increasingly difficult to find launch zones for rockets.

Tips, ideas and activities

● Children respond well to music and it can be used to reinforce a message. Words of popular songs can be re-written and sung in assembly or the children who wrote them can perform them to the school.

● Bishop Road Primary School has a number of stimulating raps on this website: www.recyclingconsortium.org.uk/schools/rubbish_raps.htm.

● Are you making enough of your bins? They may be looking a bit tired though a lick of paint should give them a bit more life. Create attractive signposts for recycling bins that are new, or aren't being used.

● Cardboard boxes, old newspapers and egg boxes are all useful resources for a classroom or for home-learning projects. However, make sure you have a safe place to store these resources – it's often useful to request them from parents only when there is a specific project. In which case you could invite parents into your class to help their child.

● The only way we are realistically going to reduce our rubbish mountain is if we use less. That is the challenge for this generation.

You Can... Recycle clothes and shoes

Recycling clothes has grown in popularity partly due to the availability of good quality, cheap clothes and partly due to good advertising by high street charity stores. Any parent can testify as to how many clothes a child can 'get through' in one year, particularly at primary age. And any school in the country will have their own clothes mountain of unclaimed lost property at the end of each term. In many ways primary schools are the natural location for a clothes bank, ensuring that these used items find a new use while providing an opportunity for the school to make a small income from the clothes company by providing this service.

Thinking points

● Each year the British public throws away over one million tonnes of clothing and household textiles - the majority of these items could either be re-used or recycled. Recycled clothes can be used in two ways.

- resold to third world countries, typically sub-Saharan African countries such as Uganda or Kenya
- processed into pulp that can be used for stuffing such as housing insulation or in stuffed envelopes.

● There is a growing market in Africa for used clothes as they lack the resources to support their own clothes manufacturing. Recycled clothes, if they are in good enough condition, provide clothing that can be resold and, importantly, employment within these countries (either to resell, wash, sort or repair old clothes). It is important to establish which country your clothes will be sold to as it is can be used as evidence of your school's link to the wider world.

Tips, ideas and activities

● Clothes recycling banks require a fair amount of space. Consult with your site manager as to where the best place is to put it. Be aware that:

- Parents will need easy access to it or it will be underused.
- The collection team will need to access it easily or it will risk not being emptied.
- You will need to monitor peak times (typically New Year and the end of the school year) when it will be full. Aim to have it emptied when it is two-thirds full to avoid bags of clothes being left on site.
- Aim to have a responsible person whose duty it is to monitor the clothes bank. The telephone number of the collection company is often printed on the side but be mindful that the company may be sited a fair distance away from your school and will need advance notice.

● Involve your school council. They will know what children want to act on first and will, importantly, spread the word for you. They are an invaluable resource and help.

● Shoe Friends is a charity that was established purely for the collection of shoes. They will provide a colourful Shoe Friends collection bin. Shoes collected through the Shoe Friends project will be reused by families living in developing countries.

● Keep families informed. Aim to write to families once a term with a 'green letter' to keep them aware of any new projects, ongoing success and any local information, such as where to find your nearest recycling facility.

● Below are a number of useful websites that could help inform how to recycle in school:
www.recycool.org
www.recycling-guide.org.uk
www.lmb.co.uk/shoefriend.html

You Can... **Recycle paper**

Paper recycling is well-established and it is likely that your school is already involved in this type of project. However, if this is not the case then recycling paper is a quick and high-profile project with which to involve your school (nobody can miss a huge paper recycling bin!)

Thinking points

● On average, for every one-metre square of recycled paper you can account for saving one tree. It is highly likely that a class will produce this amount of recycling each week, every week of the year.

● Over a third of all waste is paper. In schools and office environments that fraction is much greater. In most cases all of this paper can be recycled and yet over a third is still appearing on landfill sites.

Tips, ideas and activities

● Consider where you are going to place class collection bins. Put them somewhere that is nearer than the ordinary waste bin so that recycling paper is the easier option.

● Consider where you are going to place your main recycling bin. They are generally as large as a standard school refuse bin. As a rule of thumb you will need one bin per form so if you are a two-form primary you will most likely need two bins (though you could dedicate one for card boxes).

● Again, in the office or wherever your photocopiers are placed, make the recycling bin the nearest and therefore easiest option. Office bins may need emptying on a daily basis.

● Involve all office environments – the headteacher will need a recycling bin as much as any class. Again, encourage colleagues to place them as near to their desks as possible so that they are the easiest option.

● Avoid waste photocopying or printing. Always ask yourself the question do I need to photocopy this or can it be shown on the interactive whiteboard? Do I need to print this e-mail or can I just forward it?

● If your school has a litter team (see page 28) one of their weekly tasks could be to empty the paper bins into the main recycling bin (you may need to use Key Stage 2 buddies with the younger classes as the bins can be relatively heavy).

● Contact your local environment officer. They may be able to support or source your paper recycling project by providing bins.

● Below are a number of useful websites that could help your school to recycle more:
www.yellow-woods.co.uk (see page 32)
www.bioregional.com
www.wrap.org.uk
www.recycledproducts.org.uk

RECYCLE BIN

You Can... Recycle Yellow Pages

Each year thousands of telephone directories are discarded and put into landfill. These books are relatively easy to recycle and, as a result, a few years ago the Yellow Woods Challenge was established in partnership with the Woodlands Trust. The project runs between December and January and acts as a good 'new year's resolution' for families and local businesses.

Thinking points

● If possible, identify when the directories are going to be delivered in your area. If you advertise it too soon then enthusiasm can wane but if you advertise after delivery then households and businesses may have already thrown their old directories away.

● Consider where you are going to place your collection bin. It should be accessible for all families but not directly beneath a roof as wet directories are heavy and unpleasant. Be mindful that young children may be carrying their old directories so aim to place your collection bin/site close to the school's entrance.

● Storing what can be up to 200 directories is a challenge in itself. With your site manager, try to identify an accessible place to put them, preferably not too far away from the main collection site as moving a full bin of directories is heavy work.

Tips, ideas and activities

● Sign up to the challenge through your local authority environment officer and allocate a member of staff as the challenge coordinator.

● Tell children how to collect old Yellow Pages safely, and when and where to bring them to school.

● Write to the families explaining how the project is working and how they can support their children (by collecting directories from their place of work, setting up a collection with other families, collecting from friends and family.)

● If a child lives in a block of flats they could (with adult help) establish a recycling point. (One child in a school regularly collects over 40 Yellow Pages each year using this method.)

● Form a team to count your Yellow Pages who then update the total chart – this will keep enthusiasm going. Raise awareness of how the recycled directories can be used to make:
  - cardboard
  - animal bedding
  - home insulation
  - newspaper
  - padded envelopes and bags
  - egg cartons.

● Remind the children to collect only old directories. New directories will not be counted as part of the school's collection.

● The target figure is based on the number of directories divided by the number of children in school in order to ensure that small schools have an equal chance against larger primaries.

● Below are a number of useful websites that could support your Yellow Pages collection in school:
www.yellow-woods.co.uk
www.treeforall.org.uk

You Can... Learn the 4Rs: reduce, reuse, recycle, repair

In the 'old days' children were taught the 3Rs: reading, writing and arithmetic (of which only reading was a genuine 'R'). Today, children are exposed to a new set: the 4Rs – reduce, reuse, recycle and repair. These four words form the backbone to school environmentalism. You've done most of the hard work when your community understands what these words stand for and buy into them as an ideal. The next stage is putting them into practice.

Thinking points

● Your school is a model to your local community. The changes you make can, in time, affect dozens of families and influence environmental changes at home. When you are making changes, such as a recycling project or reducing your water use, advertise it in letters or on a notice board. You cannot underestimate the power of playground gossip and families will meet you half way if you are willing to lead the good practice.

● Of the four 'R's, 'repair' receives the least attention. We live in a throw away culture (for example, we throw away literally trillions of plastic, single use bags every year) and the concept of repair seems alien. But it is worth it. Not only can it lead to a sense of personal satisfaction but it also improves confidence. You might get it wrong the first time but your confidence will grow which, in turn, will empower you to tackle larger tasks.

Tips, ideas and activities

● Ask your class to think about which activities and projects could be placed under each of the four 'R's. This will stimulate debate as children discuss which of the four 'R's their personal ideas belong to.

● Ask children to list what 4R projects they do at home? Could they be doing more? Could they be turning off electrical items in the evening and reducing the amount of energy they use? Could they be re-using objects before throwing them away (maybe make a list of 'easy to re-use' objects)? What recycling do they do? Are they in a recycling zone? What objects have they thrown away that could have been repaired? Do they know where to go if something is broken that they want repairing?

● Do you need to provide training for parents? Many of the post baby-boomer generation (Generation X) don't have the same skills as their parents but certainly have the willingness to try. One-off courses can be useful and fun for both parents and children. Your school will be linked to a regional network called a Network Learning Community managed by a consortium of local headteachers. Funding is allocated to these networks away from the local authority and can be accessed for environmental projects if they are linked to learning or extended schooling. Often there is far less red tape and the funding should be quick to access. If your site manager is available you may want to consider running basic 'fix it' courses on Saturdays when both parents are more likely to be available.

● Below are a number of useful websites that could support 4R projects:
www.ns.ec.gc.ca/udo/reuse.html
www.buildeazy.com/kidsdiy.html
www.diykids.org
www.make-stuff.com

You Can... **Recycle mobile phones and ink cartridges**

Gone are the days when recycling meant a cardboard box in the foyer for any old books. Today there are dozens of companies that will support your school in setting up professional recycling projects that meet both an environmental agenda and can act as a funding stream in their own right. With little effort, a school can add hundreds of pounds to its budget each year through recycling.

Thinking points

● Mobile phones, ink cartridges and batteries all contain precious materials that are of value beyond their use. There is a growing market in emerging countries for older phones, and most ink cartridges can be steam-cleaned and refilled. It is important to consider: where will you will site your recycling facilities? Although a mobile phone recycling bin is relatively small, several of these can quickly clutter up a main lobby and can be a bit of an eyesore.

● With little effort a school should be able to raise £500 (a one-form entry school) to over £1000 a year through recycling. Although this can be placed directly into the main school budget it is an opportunity to create a small budget for other sustainable projects (such as buying bird or bat boxes.)

● Advertise your projects. Local newspapers are generally interested in this type of news and the knock-on effect is it promotes the school.

Tips, ideas and activities

● Try to reduce the number of ink cartridges your school uses by centralising printers. A laser printer lasts longer and is financially more efficient than an ink jet printer. Also, they can often be networked around the school so fewer are needed. Not only does this resolve the ongoing issue of not having the correct ink cartridges in stock but the printed product is of a higher quality. It's a win-win situation.

● Ink cartridges are hard to recycle but relatively easy to reuse. Families will quickly get into the habit of bringing them into the school for recycling, particularly if they feel that the school is benefiting financially.

● If you do not currently run an ink or mobile phone recycling project you could invite a recycling business to visit your school and explain to the children how their recycling can help the environment and the school and how it can, in many cases, be financially beneficial (though keep this realistic.)

● Involve your school council. They will know what children want to act on first and will, importantly, spread the word for you. They are an invaluable resource and help.

● Keep families informed. Aim to write to families once a term with a 'green letter' to keep them aware of any new projects, ongoing success and any local information, such as where to find your nearest recycling facility.

● Below are a number of useful websites that could help inform how to recycle in school:
www.recycool.org
www.recycling-guide.org.uk
www.cartridgesave.co.uk/recycling/becoming_saver_school.html
www.internet-ink.co.uk/Recycling/Recycling.htm
www.cashforcartridges.co.uk
www.recyclingconsortium.org.uk
www.recycle-more.co.uk

You Can... **Help to reduce the plastic bag mountain**

There is nothing worse in the middle of winter than seeing dozens of supermarket shopping bags caught in tree branches. It is a clear reminder that these everyday objects take years to biodegrade, during which time they become grey, are an environmental hazard and an eyesore. As a result, there is increasing pressure on supermarkets to change their policy on the distribution of plastic bags and is an area that schools can actively support. As of the 2008 Budget, supermarkets will be required to actively reduce the number of bags issued or face penalties.

Thinking points

● Over 10 billion plastic bags are used in Britain each year. They cause the deaths of over 100,000 animals and take around 400 years to biodegrade.

● The main supermarkets in France, Belgium and Scandinavia have, for several years, stopped providing free plastic bags. Instead, customers are encouraged to bring their own bags or can purchase hemp and long-life ones from the counter. It has, unsurprisingly, had little impact on their profit or the number of customers. These supermarket giants have taken the opinion that the general public are responsible enough to bring their own bags and will do so if bags are not available.

● In the UK over the last couple of years increasing pressure, both environmentally and from the public, has encouraged the reduction of free bags. The Co-op has trialled scaling down their use in selected areas, and B&Q and Marks and Spencer have enforced a 5p levy on all single-use bags.

Tips, ideas and activities

● Approaching a cloth bag company to produce book bags with the school logo on is not only a fund-raising opportunity but they are also useful for PE kits, books or shopping.

● Plastic bags can be recycled to produce school items such as rulers and protractors. These are available from general schools resource catalogues and should state that they are from recycled material.

● The environment officer should be able to source an appropriate bag collection container (similar to the ones used outside large supermarkets) for school recycling.

● As part of a literacy lesson, children or the school council could write to their local MP raising their concerns about plastic bags. An MP is obliged to write back to each child individually on House of Commons headed paper and to then pass on their comments to the appropriate Select Committee who will also reply to the school. Not only does this give children a meaningful opportunity to use their writing skills but it is a responsible use of their civil rights.

● Increasing areas of the country are becoming bag free (as inspired by Rebecca Hosking's work in Modbury, Devon). Find out whether there is a movement against plastic bags in your area.

● Below are some useful websites that could help inform how to reduce the use of plastic bags:
http://news.bbc.co.uk/1/hi/england/devon/6911780.stm
www.onyabags.co.uk
www.biobag.no

You Can... Understand the 2041 Antarctic Treaty

The Antarctic is a unique environment that is dominated by snow, cold and ice. Interestingly, because there is little snowfall it is classed as a desert. It is the last remaining continent that humans do not control. Nobody technically 'owns' the Antarctic as it was quickly recognised as being of unique scientific interest. The Madrid Protocol, signed in 1991, banned mining but this is up for review in 2041. With a land mass similar in size to Australia, there may well be untold treasures beneath the ice. The question is, should it be protected or not?

Thinking points

● The Antarctic is being affected by global warming in a dramatic way. Each year icebergs break off from the large floating ice shelves and float away into the ocean, eventually melting. This process is called calving, and it has been accelerating. As more ice calves away from the ice shelves, it exposes more sea which, unlike the ice, does not reflect heat. This acts as a feedback loop, speeding up the process of melt, which in turn creates more sea. As yet, icebergs have only been calved off from ice sheets and not the land. Unlike the Arctic, which is believed to be around 20 to 40 metres thick and floats on top of the ocean, the ice sheets of the Antarctic are closer to 2000 metres at their thickest and lie over a land mass. If these Antarctic ice sheets were to start calving into the oceans the impact on ocean levels would be felt across the world.

Tips, ideas and activities

● Research Robert Swan – an explorer and activist who has drawn the world's attention to the Antarctic. Working with the Russian Antarctic Division, he removed 1500 tonnes of rubbish and is the only man to have walked across both poles. It is as a result of his work that the E-Base, a sustainable educational centre built on King George Island, Antarctica, was established.

● It is possible to communicate with scientists on the Antarctic through the E-Base (http://ebase.2041.com). This centre is powered by solar energy and has the central aim of inspiring and educating children about the Antarctic. To date more than 20 teachers from across the world have visited the base.

● The E-Base is a sustainable green building operated in an environmentally and resource-efficient manner. The materials used to build it were very carefully selected and they include recycled and renewable resources. It is believed that a cornerstone of sustainable design is to obtain as many resources as possible from within a community however, there are no building materials produced, or indigenous supplies available, in Antarctica. E-Base went live in March 2008.

● Below are a number of web-based resources that further explain the 2041 Antarctic Treaty:
www.2041.com
www.coolantarctica.com

You Can... **Learn about biospheres**

The Eden Project in Cornwall is arguably one of the crown jewels in the country. With its space-like biomes it has attracted millions of visitors since it opened in 2000. The site comprises of three environmental biome areas, two of which are created from the space-like biospheres for plants from warmer climates. The site has a dedicated education centre, The Core, from which it runs a stimulating and exciting education programme unlike most things a child will have experienced before. It is unlikely that children or adults will forget a visit to the centre for a long time.

Thinking points

● Environmental centres such as The Eden Project, London Zoo, Butterfly World and Biota! are turning their attention away from exhibition to education. In the last few years London Zoo has been transformed into, what is essentially, a giant interactive classroom. The animals' living spaces have been dramatically improved and, for much of the zoo, it is us who are invading the animals' lives and not the other way round. For all these sites, environmental understanding and our impact on it are core messages.

● Historically, it is believed that there have been five mass extinctions on this planet. Many scientists believe that we are in the epoch of the sixth. The dilemma is that there are many species that we know little about or have rarely seen that are rapidly dying out. We simply don't know the whole picture. Our children both deserve and need to understand this is a fragile Earth.

Tips, ideas and activities

● An Eden Project visit needs good planning if you are going to make best use of the site. Their website will explain how your school can make the most of your visit.

● Both your children and families will need preparation before the site visit. Your school will, most likely, have an educational visit risk assessment form. If you do not have one then ask your educational visits coordinator. Ensure that:
  ● Your booking does not coincide with other events such as parents' consultation night or key twilight training.
  ● You book in advance, generally three months is a good rule of thumb. This will ensure you have a booking date and will give you time to organise transport.
  ● One month before the visit, you meet with the adult helpers to guide them through the visit's aims and identified risks. At this point aim to have a clear idea of your groups and who is leading each group.
  ● If you have new adult volunteers they do not necessarily need to have a CRB check but will need a List 99 check. The details you will need are name (including maiden name), date of birth and place of residence. The check can be done by the borough (your educational visits coordinator should have the appropriate name) and should take less than 24 hours.

● A similar dome site called Butterfly World is scheduled to open by 2011 in St Albans, Hertfordshire. The £25m tropical bubble will contain more than 250,000 butterflies on a 26–acre site. Its centrepiece will be a dome which will house tropical butterfly species from around the world.

● Below are a number of useful websites that could help your school find out about or plan visits to different projects:
www.edenproject.com
www.butterfly-world.org
www.zsl.org/zsl-london-zoo
www.zsl.org/biota

You Can... **Learn about climate change**

It would be hard to ignore the fact that climatic changes are occurring and the effects that they are having on our country and daily lives. Tornados in London, blistering summers, flooding in the West Country and North East, water spouts off Wales and record warm temperatures are becoming commonplace events. Even the most conservative cannot overlook the reality of ripe blackberries in mid-November and that the lawn needs mowing in February. So what does this mean for our children and their future?

Thinking points

- It is important to understand that climate change is a result of global warming. In effect, one is the symptom of the other. It is also worth noting that there has always been and always will be climate change. The difference at this moment in time is the seemingly rapid severity of it.

- It is widely believed that the Earth has undergone at least five mass extinctions all of which have been, in one way or another, linked to extreme climate change brought on by either global warming or cooling (an effect referred to as 'Snowball Earth'). In all cases the Earth has fully recovered and new life has sprung from where the old once existed and there is increasing evidence to suggest that such a mass extinction is upon us. So, in hard terms it is not the Earth we should be worried about. It's us.

Tips, ideas and activities

- As with any major event it is best to prepare children for what might lie ahead for them, without being too alarmist. They will hear of climate news almost daily and there is good evidence to suggest that children are less anxious and feel more prepared for the future when schools address climate issues head on.

- Within this book there are many suggestions for how to address children's learning about climate change but the very least, and most effective task, you can do is write to your local Member of Parliament. It is their duty to take your letter seriously. Equally it can offer a real opportunity for children to write to their MP with a genuine concern. In this case they will not only be learning about a world-wide issue but doing something positive about it.

- The BBC and Royal Society have put together on their websites a digest of the facts and fiction that surrounds climate change. They are quick and useful websites aimed at non-specialists (see below).

- Increasingly, climate change is linked with carbon neutral projects. Although this is reasonable when considering options to reduce our carbon emissions and therefore our aims to stem the changes to our climate, it is not just carbon that is of concern. Other gases such as methane are far more potent greenhouse gases and the effects of global warming are unlocking these gases from permafrost regions, such as Siberia, and releasing them into our atmosphere. That said, we all have a responsibility to reduce our carbon footprint and if we all managed to change one thing, the knock-on effect could be global.

- Below are a number of useful websites about climate change:
www.dft.gov.uk/ActOnCO2
www.google.co.uk/carbonfootprint
www.royalsociety.org/climatechange

You Can... Investigate the impact of pollution

There is no other species that has, in the history of the Earth, had such an impact on this planet as we have. Quite simply we have polluted the skies, the water and much of the land. Barely 5% of the planet is untouched by our pollution. It's quite an achievement considering we managed to do most of this in only 150 years. Where will we be in 150 years time and what will this planet look like?

Thinking points

● The global number one energy user, and therefore carbon consumer, is America. As a nation it has refused to sign up to scientifically based agreements, such as the Kyoto Treaty of 1999. That said, dozens of individual US states have turned away from corporate America and are independently signing the treaty and developing robust environmental policies to counter their states' environmental impact. It is an important step in the right direction.

● There are locations across the seas and oceans that are referred to as 'dead zones'. Nothing lives in dead zones because the oxygen has been starved out of the water. In places this is partly as a result of plastics forming a tiny film across the water's surface and blocking oxygenation of the water.

Tips, ideas and activities

● It is easy to be overpowered by the enormous task that is ahead of us but pollution is continuing to have a devastating impact on our globe and the only way to stop this is to dispose of our rubbish in a responsible way. Consider what recycling and waste disposal projects you are running.

● There are two main categories of pollution: water and air. Air pollutants travel furthest and have long-term consequences but water-based pollutants tend to have the most aggressive short-term results (for example, an oil tanker spill or acid rain).

● Visit a local stream or wet area. A wildlife study should reveal if the water is polluted or not. Typically, the water should be clear and relatively weed-free. There may be a local river centre that can offer expert support and advice. Your local wildlife trust may also organise educational days on pond-dipping, being an eco-warrior, and so on.

● Ask children to share what they know about pollution. Do they understand about chemical pollution, aerosols, oil and acids (as found in batteries or mobile phones)?

● We can do something about pollution. In the 1980s a successful ban on CFCs (chlorofluorocarbons) brought about the reduction in a gigantic ozone 'hole' above Australia. Yet, ironically in the early 1900s when CFCs were first invented they were heralded as a great discovery and earned the scientist a Nobel Prize. Interestingly, the scientist who pinpointed the link between the ozone depletion and CFCs (and then successfully recommended their ban) was also awarded the Nobel Prize.

● Below are a number of useful websites that could support projects to raise awareness of pollution:
www.oceansidecleanwaterprogram.org/kids.asp
http://tiki.oneworld.net
www.silentscourge.com/Children_and_Pollution.html
www.wildlifetrusts.org

You Can... Go fair trade

Fair trade products have moved from the niche market and are now mainstream with more and more large producers adopting a 'fair trade only' approach. The Co-op has been, for a long time, the flag bearer for this movement but fair trade products are increasingly available from most major supermarket chains. With competitive prices and competitive quality, the question is 'Why not go fair trade?'

Thinking points

● Fair trade involves a conscious decision of change. It has been likened to lifestyle choices or the consumer making a soft political stand but at its heart is a simple message: a fair price for a fair product. Many farmers in developing and third world markets struggle to provide for their families. Poor access to markets and traders means that they are open to exploitation. Fair trade seeks to guarantee a better deal for farmers and workers in the developing world.

Tips, ideas and activities

● Do you drink coffee or tea? Do you like sugar with it? The answers are probably, if staffrooms across the world are anything to go by, yes. Fairly traded products are becoming more competitively priced and can be considered as a replacement in the staffroom. Indeed Tate and Lyle, the sugar company, will only be producing fairly traded sugar products from 2009 – so there's no excuse!

● Raise the profile of fair trade by running a fair trade stall at your school fairs and by selling fair trade products in the school tuck shop. The Fairtrade Foundation website gives information on how schools can get involved, how to order promotional material, and how to apply to become a fair trade school.

● Fair trade can touch many areas of the curriculum: in geography find out where different fair trade products come from and compare the localities; in maths, compare prices of fair trade and non-fair trade products and explore how much more workers get paid if they are involved in fair trade.

● Investigate the range of products under the fair trade logo. The list has grown rapidly over the last 10 years and includes coffee, tea, herbal teas, chocolate, cocoa, sugar, bananas, grapes, pineapple, dried fruits, juices and smoothies, biscuits, cakes, snacks, honey, chutneys, rice, wine, nut oils, ale, confectionery, flowers. How many of these are used in school or by children at home?

● Below are a number of useful websites that could support fair trade projects in school:
www.fairtrade.org.uk
www.fairtradeatwork.org.uk

You Can... **Work with your site manager**

The days of the old-style school caretaker are quickly drawing to a close. More often this role is now, in a far more expanded form, being replaced by site managers or site business leaders. This expanded role now encompasses the development and care of the school site, often including duties to report to governors, the headteacher and local authority. As the manager of the site, they are best placed to support any physical environmental changes.

Thinking points

● The site manager should be familiar with the latest building environmental requirements. This will help inform any developments that you are considering making to the site and can add weight to proposals: for example, replacing windows with double glazing may be a short-term expense but could reap long-term savings in energy costs.

● Using a site manager either as a consultant or guest in school council meetings can help to unveil their job. They are in a unique position within school in so much as that they are a senior member of staff but one who is not directly connected to learning. This can provide a genuine opportunity for children to learn about other forms of employment, while working with a familiar adult. It also adds value to the contribution this adult makes, thereby reinforcing their position within the school.

Tips, ideas and activities

● Conducting an energy survey or environmental survey could be done in partnership with the site manager. They know the school and can access data that will enable any environmental survey to be completed as fully as possible.

● Link your site manager to an eco-group, such as an energy team. He or she will have access to the data an energy team may require if they are measuring the quantity of energy consumed by the school. Equally, they will value working with this familiar individual on a professional basis.

● If you are considering any major site developments, your site manager will be able to source appropriate quotes and line- manage the project on your behalf. It is a general rule of thumb that you should secure three quotes if a project is over £5000. These can be delegated to the site manager to source.

● Your site manager can act as a spokesperson on your behalf when addressing governors in premises meetings, which are often held at times that are difficult for teachers to attend.

● Involving your site manager will add value to their position; the children will appreciate it, as will they.

You Can... Review the school site

Reviewing the grounds, both inside and out, is a key part of your environmental review. If possible, review the site with an outside expert (the local authority school environment officer, a network school colleague, the site manager or a link partner from the Woodland Trust) as you can then pool ideas. The review should then help you to identify what action might be needed against the seven core environmental themes: water, litter, energy, waste (recycling), transport, healthy living and biodiversity.

Thinking points

- Looking afresh at your site is an ideal opportunity to re-evaluate your playground provision. It is possible to develop a sustainable school site that equally supports children's play (nearly a quarter of a child's day is spent out in the playground). Things to consider could be micro-allotments, an accessible composter, an external energy monitor, insect habitats (such as lace-wing or ladybird boxes) that can create outside learning opportunities.

- Some parts of reaching a basic environmental level are either cheap or free to implement (such as water butts, wormeries, bug-boxes or tree planting). However there are others, such as solar panel installation or, if it is appropriate, the installation of a wind turbine, that are more costly. It is important to add these items to your environmental vision with the increasing availability of energy grants. Sustained energy reduction is not free which, in itself, is a useful learning point for children.

Tips, ideas and activities

- If your school is within a Network Learning Community (a cluster of primary and secondary schools that are local to your area), skills and expertise can be shared across it. An NLC partner school may have already undergone a site review and could offer support and guidance.

- A site survey should form part of your environmental action plan. A complete plan may look overwhelming. However, aim to focus on one key area at a time. It is straightforward advice but it is better to improve one area of the school grounds and thereby gain support than to try and fail to complete too many projects in one year.

- When surveying your site, questions to consider are:
  - Does the school recycle garden or fruit/vegetable waste in a composter or wormery?
  - Do you ever hold lessons or parts of lessons outside? Are you able to?
  - Have pupils explored into the heritage of the school grounds?
  - What proportion of the school boundaries are hedges, trees, wire, open? How could boundaries be improved to encourage plants and wildlife?
  - What proportion of the school's grounds are grass, tarmac, woodland, hedgerow, water or wetland, play areas, flower beds, seating areas, conservation areas or wildlife centre? How could these be improved?

- Below are a number of useful websites that could support a site review:
  www.playgroundpartnerships.org
  www.teachernet.gov.uk/docbank/index.cfm?id=9046
  www.kentsport.org/schools/SchoolSport_
  PlaygroundDevelopment.cfm
  www.solar4schools.co.uk
  www.carbontrust.co.uk
  www.woodland-trust.org.uk

You Can... **Plant a tree**

National Tree Week is an event at the end of November that has been led by The Tree Council (UK) since 1975. Schools across the country are invited to take part in this event, either at school or at a nearby conservation area, to plant trees and other similar habitat-creating vegetation. The Tree Council has, as its core aims, four principles:

- *making trees matter to everyone*
- *more trees of the right kind, in the right places*
- *better care for all trees, of all ages*
- *inspiring effective action for trees.*

Thinking points

- You may well have conducted a site audit and if so should have identified how well your trees are aging. Old trees should be replaced and The Tree Council can offer good advice on what sorts of trees to plant. It does not necessarily mean that you should replace like for like trees as there may well be more suitable ones for the conditions offered on your site. Schools within a conservation zone should consult with their local council conservation officer when replacing trees.

- If you have limited space you may want to consider planting a hedgerow. Hedges are in great decline across the country and offer a wonderful habitat for all sorts of animals. It is also an opportunity for a wider group of the school community to be involved as children can each plant individual hedge 'whips'.

Tips, ideas and activities

- Planting hedges and trees is a long process. In order to give children a sense of achievement, consider planting bulbs or wild flowers. This will also involve more children and support a diverse habitat.

- Trees, as a resource, are habitats. To maximise this, attach lace-wing and ladybird boxes to them. Along with bird boxes this will quickly create a diverse habitat that not only supports the local wildlife but is an active example of the food chain and so can be incorporated into the school's science curriculum.

- The Woodland Trust is very willing to support schools and children with a wide range of activities that work alongside tree planting. They offer a tree pack that contains a whole range of activities, stickers, challenges and promotions supporting tree and wood conservation. If your school is close to a Woodland Trust site it is well worth creating a link, if you have not done so already, as they often run special events in partnership with wildlife experts. If you have the stamina, children love the summer evening bat watches.

- The charity Tree For All, a charity, offers free trees for schools. School grounds in need of TLC can benefit from a free pack of 30 native trees (enough for a small grove or short length of hedge), which come with guidance on planting and maintenance plus curriculum-linked activities.

- Below are a number of useful websites that could help support tree conservation in your school:
www.treecouncil.org.uk
www.woodland-trust.org.uk
www.naturedetectives.org.uk/club
www.treeforall.org.uk

You Can... Install micro-allotments

Whether you use pots, allotments, gardens, pocket plots, or orchards it is the process of growing that is important: this enables children to understand where their food comes from and can lead on to discussion of related issues, such as food miles and ethical farming. Simply living in the countryside is no longer an assurance that children will have the opportunity to grown their own food. The DfES therefore developed the Growing Schools website (www.teachernet.gov.uk/growingschools), which is designed to support schools with the 'outside classroom', particularly focusing on food, farming and the countryside.

Thinking points

● Working through the process of planting, watering, tendering and harvesting is not only productive it is also satisfying and children take great pride in presenting (and then consuming) the fruit or vegetables that they have grown. The smallest plot will be given as much love as any larger one.

● It is important that what the children are growing should have a realistic element of success and it is worth obtaining advice from either keen gardening parents or the local garden centre on what to plant. Not being able to grow something can leave children feeling that they don't have 'green fingers' when this should not be the case.

● Take time to consider where children can plant around your school site so that a range of opportunities are available for different children. This may include plant pots, micro-allotments, bulb sites or walls for creepers.

Tips, ideas and activities

● 'Pocket plots' are a fun way to introduce younger children to growing. A large plastic container lid (such as from a coffee jar) lined with tissue paper and kept moist provides a good environment for cress and mustard seeds. In around 14 days children will have a pocket pot that can either be harvested or decorated with small items to make a garden.

● Pots are a useful and space-friendly way to involve children in gardening. They are ideal spaces for plants that require little attention other than regular watering such as flowering bulbs, strawberries (though they require specialised pots) or common herbs such as chive, mint, sage or basil.

● Micro-allotments are an affordable and realistic way for schools with little space or no green space to grow their own fruit and vegetables. Available online or from most garden centres, micro-allotments are essentially large plastic containers that act like an enlarged pot. Place the allotment out of direct sunlight and line it with stones. Then fill it with earth and top it with good compost (you could use your own compost) before planting. The advantage of micro-allotments over pots is that root vegetables (potatoes, carrots) and vine vegetables (pumpkin, runner beans) have more space to grow. The growing space is manageable for a class who can also personalise the allotment.

● Generally potatoes, sunflowers, strawberries and tomatoes grow under most conditions.

● Bulbs need little support and if you have a nearby wall, consider planting a creeper such as wisteria or ivy.

● Below are two useful websites that could help inform, resource and develop a sustainable growing area:
www.allotment.org.uk
www.schoolsgarden.org.uk

You Can... Create play zones

Around a quarter of a child's school life is spent in the playground but, historically, this area has been poorly resourced and underused as a learning space. However, in recent years schools have been able to access considerable funding – through grants such as the Big Lottery Fund or, more recently, the Primary Strategy for Change. These have allowed the types of facelift that, as children, we could only dream of.

Thinking points

● Schools have a responsibility to provide adequate shelter from the increasingly extreme elements: January 2008 was one of the wettest January's on record and eight out of the last ten years have been the hottest recorded.

● It is possible to obtain shelters from a school travel plan grant if it has the dual use of a waiting area for either parents or children at the end of the day and more grants are becoming available for this provision. Your local school travel advisor will be able to support grant applications and usually will complete the paperwork on your behalf.

Tips, ideas and activities

● Evaluate your play space. If you don't have a garden, where could you place one? (see micro-allotments, p44) If you do have a garden, how could you enhance this learning space to create opportunities for children to experience different habitats? Involve the children in the redevelopment of your playground – it is their space, after all. If you have a budget or are working towards a grant, be realistic about what you can afford but also keep in mind that simple reorganisation of the site can have as big an impact as a totally new playground.

● Dividing the playground into zones can rationalise the space. Football pitches do not need to be the full length of the playground and more, smaller zones can offer a wider range of sporting opportunities. Consider planning for:
  ● mini football pitches
  ● mini basketball areas
  ● skipping zones
  ● line markings for square ball, hand tennis, hopscotch (consider using different markings instead of 1–10, such as hand signs or numbers in a different alphabet)
  ● use your walls – these can be converted into any number of target games
  ● quiet spaces for calmer activities such as cat's cradle.

● Timetable zones – this will avoid one group of children dominating one particular zone and will encourage children to try different activities during the week.

● Develop a gardening space. Children enjoy gardening, even if it is at break times. A meal supervisor may be happy to lead 30 minutes of daily gardening. This will also reduce the number of children in the main playground.

● The websites below can offer more support for developing a gardening area or play zones:
www.kidsgardening.com
www.bbc.co.uk/gardening/gardening_with_children/
www.fairplaytraining.org.uk/play_gettingactive.htm

You Can... Employ playground buddies

Children are a wonderful resource to use within the playground and will be keen, if given the chance, to support break times by being a play friend. It is also a chance for children to fulfil the Every Child Matters outcome by making a positive contribution.

Thinking points

● Buddies can model good practice, such as putting litter in bins, vegetation in composters (fruit peel or cores) and modelling how to play within the environment harmoniously. They can also introduce younger children to gardening by sharing skills with small groups.

● Starting a playground buddy or playground friends scheme is a commitment that requires time, organisation, people skills, professional development and ongoing management. It is not to be entered into lightly. That said, when it works – and it might not the first time around – it can double the number of useful people in the playground and give the older children a genuine purpose.

Tips, ideas and activities

● It is important to involve the lunchtime supervisors; the children should understand that they are part of a larger team.

● Invite children from Years 5 and 6 to complete and send in an application form. Explain that questions must be answered honestly. Your application form may include questions such as:
  ● Why have you applied for this job?
  ● Which of your qualities would make you a good buddy?
  ● What experience do you have of working with younger children?
  ● What skills would you use in the playground or classroom (if it is a wet break)?
  ● What would you do if you saw two children arguing?

● Follow up an application with an interview. This may seem formal but it adds the necessary weight to the job that makes children want to have it and gives them a wonderful experience that is beyond the curriculum. Interview questions should reflect those used in the application and an interview should last no longer than five minutes. Ensure that you write to each child, informing them of the panel's decision.

● At the first meeting, ask the children to form five groups (Mon–Fri) taking into account a gender balance and whether they have lunchtime activities on certain days. Photograph each group. This is important as it advertises their faces to the younger children.

● Initially you may want to station them around the playground. A child near the grassed area can support play that does not damage the plants, for example.

● Make time to have a weekly meeting with the buddies and aim to have one piece of training such as a new game.

● Regularly review the buddies with the meal supervisors. Invite them to identify a 'Buddy of the Week'.

● These websites could help establish playground friends in your school:
www.playgroundpartnerships.org
www.playgroundfriends.co.uk

You Can... **Build a school for the future**

With the Building Schools for the Future building programme and Primary Strategy for Change on the horizon there has never been a better time to address the environmental impact of your school. There are genuine opportunities to re-build your school and its environment within the primary and secondary sectors. Obviously this will not be the case for all schools but a baseline assessment of what should be expected by our pupils in a 21st century school site is currently being undertaken. This will go towards ensuring a basic environmental equality across all schools.

Thinking points

● If sustainable schools are to become a reality, it will require commitment from school leadership and the community as buildings will achieve little on their own. When schools are considering improvements to their site they must also consider what systems and working practices must also change to make the most of the new investment.

● It goes without saying that school staff know their school best. This has been acknowledged by the House of Commons Education and Skills Committee who have recommended that teachers, other school staff and pupils must be involved in the planning processes for redevelopment projects. If you are not involved, then get involved. It may take longer for the development to take place but the invested time will contribute to the success of the project.

Tips, ideas and activities

● Typically, school leaders are not used to the process of building. Few new schools were built during the last third of the 20th century and investment in school sites has been historically poor. If you have not been involved with a large-scale project it is worth consulting with a local school leader who has had this experience.

● School communication is vital for health and safety, and expectation. Within the school, set up 'site development' as a regular agenda item during the period of change. Add it to the headteacher's newsletter and school/family notice boards.

● Once a project has been announced, expectation must be managed. Do not raise too much expectation until the budget, plans, contractor and timescales have been agreed. It is far easier to discuss potential once a building is complete than to backtrack on raised anticipation.

● Site development requires thought, time and continually evolving systems. Ensure from the start there are clear lines of communication between the school, borough and contractor.

● Projects often take longer than expected. Manage this carefully. There is a fine line between sharing every delay and keeping the community informed.

● Once a project is complete, the borough and contractor have a responsibility to undertake any snagging. Snagging is where defects become apparent once the building is in use, such as cracked windows, heating problems, etc. With new buildings it is often difficult to anticipate future problems during design and your snagging agreement should ensure that any of these problems are addressed and resolved.

● See www.teachernet.gov.uk for further information about the Primary Strategy for Change funding.

You Can... # Conduct a school travel survey

Understanding how your school community travel to school and then identifying how they would like to travel to school is core to being able to write a meaningful school travel plan in partnership with your local school travel advisor. Travel surveys can be conducted individually or as a 'hands up' exercise but should be done twice a year in order to assess impact.

Thinking points

● There are a wide range of surveys available (including a photocopiable one on page 62) but consider who will be filling them in. Younger children should be supported appropriately and the language should be tailored to their level. Clear instructions on how to conduct 'hands up' activities should be given (for example, 'I am going to read a set of choices so you know what they are. When I read them the second time you put your hand up once for the one you feel you agree with most.')
● Interpreting and collecting the data from surveys is often the most challenging task. It is likely that your school travel advisor will be able to do this for you. If that is not possible then consider conducting 'hands up' surveys as they are easier to interpret than individual surveys. Though they lack the individual pin-point accuracy of individual surveys, they should offer enough robust evidence to support your travel plan.

Tips, ideas and activities

● It is possible to extract the postcodes from your school database. Your school travel advisor should have access to mapping tools that can map your catchment area. This will help you to identify reasonable figures for either walking or cycling schemes.

● Involve older children in the analysis of the data. Not only is it a real-life opportunity to use number-based programs such as Excel but further involves them in the whole process. It is also an opportunity for older children to present and explain the data to the school or governors.

● There are a number of free online websites that can create surveys on your behalf. These sites will process and display the information immediately. This can save hours of counting! For an example of an online survey go to www.surveymonkey.com.

● Ensure that your evidence is available. This can be done as a display of charts and tables; a letter to families; a presentation to the school. This will keep your travel plan within the community's attention and ensure that future surveys will provide accurate information.

● Travel habits change. As a result it is important to regularly update your survey. It is recommended that you conduct a travel survey twice a year: the first survey should identify areas for action and the second should provide evidence of impact.

● Below are a number of useful websites that could support carrying out a travel survey:
www.bedfordshire.gov.uk/TransportAndStreets/SchoolTravelInitiatives/SchoolTravelSurvey.aspx
www.saferoutestoschools.org.uk/?p=tk27

You Can... **Walk to school**

Historically, primary schools have had tight catchment areas of less than a mile, unlike their secondary partners. Yet a surprisingly large number of families still opt to drive to school. This may be for any number of good reasons (and your travel survey should point this out) but there will still be an arguable number of families who could conceivably walk to school rather than drive. These are the groups that you should aim to target.

Thinking points

● Why walk? Any commuter or parent will tell you that driving near schools around the early morning drop-off or evening pick-up times adds a noticeable amount of time to your journey. Added to this, schools can seriously reduce their carbon footprint by encouraging families to walk to school rather than drive. Even if this is only one day a week, in real terms that is a 20% reduction in car journeys to school.

● If you are launching a walking scheme you may want to consider investing in high-visibility vests to keep children safer during the darker months. Grants can be given for these through the school travel plan, or your school PSA/PTA may support the costs for parents.

Tips, ideas and activities

● Schools can access postcodes via their school database. An analysis of this will give you a clearer understanding of the geographic spread of families across your catchment area. For this reason it is important to try to locate postcodes before children fill in their travel survey so that you can match surveys with geographic location.

● Park and stride is a convenient method for families who live a considerable distance from schools. The strategy is to encourage drivers to park a reasonable distance from school rather than dropping children off at the gates. This not only enables children to take part in walking events but it also reduces the congestion around the school entrance.

● Walk Once a Week (WOW) has been a hugely successful project running in London. Children each have a mini calendar that they fill in when they walk to school. If a child walks to school at least once a week during the month they receive a themed badge for that particular month. The project was developed to encourage children and families who live within a reasonable distance to try walking to school. Many schools have seen dramatic differences in school travel habits. For example, the number of children walking to school before WOW in one north London school was 22%. Four months into the project, that had leapt to 75% of children walking once a week and that figure was sustained to the end of the project and beyond.

● Below are a number of useful websites that could help inform, resource and develop walking as an alternative form of travel in your school:
www.safe-kids-walking.com
www.walktoschool.org.uk
www.walkingbus.com
www.thewalkingbus.co.uk
www.brightkidz.co.uk

You Can... Cycle to school

Cycling is increasingly becoming a fun, healthy and environmentally friendly way to get to school in preference to the car. Urban environments are often well-catered for cyclists, despite the traffic, with increasingly improved cycle lanes and cycle only zones (the charity Sustrans was awarded £50 million from the National Lottery to spend on improving and enhancing the UK's cycle lane system.)

Thinking points

● Before you start a cycling project consider the space you have for cycle storage. If you do not have any storage then you should be eligible for financial support if you include cycling within your school travel plan. Cycle storage should be both accessible and secure.

● Be mindful of any possible building works the school may have planned for in the medium future. The site you have seen as ideal for cycle storage may be under consideration for another use. Consult with your finance and premises committee before agreeing to plans.

● Cycle storage can have a double impact on the school if solar tiles are attached. It is an additional cost but the message it is presenting is clear: we are a school that is working towards full sustainability.

Tips, ideas and activities

● Contact the local police station and set up a cycle registration event. They will come to your school and, free of charge, will register any bicycle and place it onto their website (they will often supply free locks and lights to any child or adult who has brought their bike to school.)

● Hold bike events (with parental permission) such as 'bling your bike' where children can bring their bikes to school to decorate. In addition, run a 'bike2school' poster competition. This will involve children who do not have bikes in the project.

● Training a member of staff to become a cycle instructor is relatively inexpensive and also enables you to run regular school cycle clubs (cycling breakfast clubs are a fun way to get children cycling when the roads are quiet). As a nationally recognised accreditation, it is a good piece of Continuing Professional Development (CPD).

● Create a 'borrow a bike' scheme where a child who, for any number of reasons, does not have their own bike can borrow one from school. Again, grants are available through the school travel plan, extended schools provision or breakfast club business plans.

● Create a bike team to monitor the number of bikes stored at school. Identify a key day, Friday for example, that children know will be the day the team counts any bikes. It will encourage cycling on at least one day.

● Schools should aim to have 10% of its community cycling to school.

● Below are a number of useful websites that could support cycling projects in school:
www.gobike.org
www.bikeit.co.uk
www.sustrans.org.uk
www.cycletraining.co.uk

You Can... **Car pool**

It was not that long ago that car pooling was commonplace. With cars becoming cheaper to buy and more roads being built, this form of shared transport is at risk of being forgotten. Yet, it not only makes good environmental sense, it can be socially rewarding and help build better relationships with families, children or colleagues. Used in conjunction with other transport projects, car pooling can make a genuine contribution to a school's travel plan.

Thinking points

● Road congestion was so great in 2000 that vehicles were travelling slower in London than one hundred years earlier. In a bid to address this, Mayor Ken Livingstone introduced a model that has now been replicated across the world in other major cities: a congestion charge. Although there have been many critics, this form of charging has helped to reduce the volume of traffic in city centres across the country and encouraged more people than ever to cycle or walk.

● Consider the impact of one less journey a week. If you drive to work and manage to car pool once a week, the impact can be a 20% reduction in both your fuel use and carbon emissions. Given the prices of petrol it makes both financial and environmental sense.

Tips, ideas and activities

● There are a number of relatively inexpensive mapping programmes available that will take a list of postcodes and map out their spread. The postcodes can be extracted from you school's management system (your school travel advisor should be able to perform this task on your behalf.) This will show the distance people travel and should identify clusters of families who could car pool.

● Colleagues often need little encouragement to car pool but it is worth reviewing. Aside from being environmentally friendly the car is one of those rare spaces where colleagues can chat.

● There is a financial incentive to car pool. Petrol prices have soared in recent years and are set to continue as oil tips over the $100 a barrel mark (which is seen by many analysts as a key tipping point). By reducing the quantity of car journeys, colleagues are able to save on their fuel costs and until electric, hybrid or hydrogen cars fall in price, petrol will continue to be an expensive monthly financial cost.

● Consider why you are driving. Is it because you are carrying your laptop back and forth from work? If so, invest in a memory stick. For less than £30 an 8GB memory stick will hold all of your files, which you can then transport between school and home in your pocket. Is it the distance? If you live less than five miles away from school then you should seriously consider either cycling or walking. It is environmentally friendly and a guaranteed way of getting your 30 minutes of daily exercise.

● Below are a number of useful websites that could support car pooling in school:
www.carshare.com
www.car-pool.co.uk
www.nationalcarshare.co.uk

You Can... Make your school car-safe

Two of the riskiest and busiest periods of the day are during drop-off and pick-up times. At these times there are hundreds of children, dozens of adults and row upon row of cars all jostling amongst each other. It is a recipe that can lead to disaster with near misses on a daily basis. In larger schools, the pick-up period is closer to an hour as keen parents arrive early. And for schools it is a grey area of involvement with a high risk of road rage. So, what can be done?

Thinking points

● Road accidents are the number one killer for young people aged between 10 and 24, and have been for every year this century. It is a frightening statistic and one that should be taken seriously. Consider what road training your school offers? In the 1970s every school-aged child would have been involved with the Tufty Club (www.rospa.com/tufty) and although that idea is outdated, its values are not. Road safety training does not have to take much curriculum time and is a life skill. Your allocated police link will be able to help you organise training.

● You will know your environment. Where are the popular crossings? Are these crossings sufficiently marked? Does your school have a road safety sign on its main road? (You will be surprised how many schools do not, particularly older schools) Where are the 'hot spots'? How congested is the front of your school?

Tips, ideas and activities

● Do parents park on the restricted zone outside your school? If they do then they are breaking the law and to enforce this you will need the police. Community Officers have the appropriate powers and skills to manage these situations. As a grey area, schools should not expose themselves to what will be heated or persuasive arguments from parents.

● Every three years, the school travel advisor must re-write the school travel plan. It is an opportunity to stand back and look at what has been achieved and what has arisen as a result. Consider your extended location and the routes children take to school. Are they safe? If not, what do they need to be safe? Do not be afraid to impose speed restrictions around your school. Increasingly, schools are demanding 20mph zones and it is currently being debated within Parliament whether inner city and built-up areas should all be 20mph.

● Train your children. Every child under the age of five should have received their Road Safety Pack: a fun pack of stickers and activities. However, road safety needs to be reinforced in schools. Packs should also be available through local Children's Centres (see below for website.) If you are re-modelling your playground, then consider a road system so that, from as early as possible, young children are aware that road safety is linked to responsibility. Older children should have road safety reinforced. Unfortunately, unless a child in Key Stage 2 is involved with cycle training it is unlikely that they will have had any road safety training at all in their school life.

● Below are a number of useful websites that could support road safety in school:
www.thinkroadsafety.gov.uk
www.hedgehogs.gov.uk
www.surestart.gov.uk/surestartservices/settings/surestartchildrenscentres

You Can... **Apply for awards and grants**

A growing number of private, charity and state sectors are offering grants and awards to schools that are willing to demonstrate a creativity with environmental projects. Often private companies will have a particular angle on their award or grant. For example, Woolworths has an award focused on playgrounds, while B&Q has a focus on habitats and energy.

Thinking points

- Award applications take a varying amount of time to complete. They may require core school data, a timetable of project milestones, a copy of your school budget and last OFSTED report as well as evidence of review procedures. The clearer you are about your project's details, the better. Do your homework, particularly about any costs. If you believe there will be staffing costs find out how much that will be. The same can be said for any material costs. The award panel want to see that you have control of your project and that the money will be spent wisely.

- Be smart with projects. One set of funding will, in all likelihood, not be enough. Aim to match funding with other grants. If your school has a shared vision for the project then raising funds is a necessary, and important, aspect of seeing this vision through.

Tips, ideas and activities

- Below are a range of grants available to schools. It is worth contacting your local environment officer who should be able to direct you to new funding.

- **Awards for All**
  Grants of between £300 and £10,000 are available for people to take part in art, sport, heritage and community activities, and projects that promote education, the environment and health in the local community. www.awardsforall.org.uk

- **E.ON Source Fund for Renewable Energy Projects**
  The E.ON Source Fund supports community energy projects that either result in the production of energy from a sustainable source or that reduce the amount of energy used by a community organisation. Grants of up to £30,000 are available to community groups, charities and not-for-profit organisations across England, Scotland and Wales. www.eon-uk.com/about/2688.aspx

- **Eco-Schools' Switched on Communities**
  Applications for grants up to a maximum of £5000 are considered for new or existing projects that create positive change and development within a school on the themes of energy and water. Priority will be given to projects that clearly demonstrate an energy efficiency element or identify technology solutions for environmental improvements. www.eco-schools.org.uk

- **B&Q's One Planet Living Awards**
  B&Q is offering awards of between £1000 and £10,000 (€1500 and €15,000 in the Republic of Ireland) of its products to voluntary organisations in its new One Planet Living Awards for 2008. B&Q is also offering two awards of £5,000 combined cash/product to schools who submit 'innovative science-based proposals.' www.diy.com/awards

You Can... Go carbon neutral

There is a lot of discussion about our carbon footprint. So much so that 'what a carbon footprint is' has become clouded by what it stands for. In essence, a carbon footprint is a measure of our emissions against our energy use (such as vehicles, gas, electricity and water). The Carbon Trust was established to support public and private sectors to offset their carbon measures (also known as carbon footprint) with sustainable energy devices or energy reduction ideas.

Thinking points
● The Carbon Trust has a clear mission statement, which is 'to accelerate the move to a low carbon economy by working with organisations to reduce carbon emissions and develop commercial low carbon technologies'. Although schools are not businesses they do control a substantial budget that comes directly from the tax payer. It is their duty to ensure that the budget is being spent wisely. Making energy saving changes to the school can work towards this.

● UK schools could reduce energy costs by around £20 million a year, which would prevent 300,000 tonnes of CO_2 from entering the atmosphere. (Source: The Carbon Trust).

● The UK water industry consumes around 3% of the total energy used in the UK. Getting drinkable tap water is not free – it requires energy in treatment and pumping. Fix that leaky tap!

Tips, ideas and activities
● The Carbon Trust (www.carbontrust.co.uk) has a range of energy grants that schools can access. Generally these are match-funded grants.

● Heat only those areas you need to heat. Aim to warm rooms by the time people enter them but then cool them down during the day. They will retain their heat well into the evening. Recommended temperatures are 18°C for normal teaching, 15°C for shared walking spaces such as corridors and 21°C for special needs schools, low activity areas or areas with very young children.

● Maintain your boiler and pipework; check your thermostats.

● Deal with leaky taps and fit percussion taps, which turn off automatically.

● Insulate hot water tanks and their distribution pipes.

● Undertake regular maintenance.

● Improve your glazing.

● Replace failing light bulbs and lamps and avoid 'blinds down and lights on'.

● Purchase catering equipment with running costs in mind. Always look for the energy efficiency rating.

● Add timers to plugs to ensure that they are switched off overnight. Switch off equipment if it is not being used.

● Check your equipment regularly. Schools should annually PAT (Portable Appliance Test) test electrical equipment.

● The Carbon Trust has a selection of useful booklets available on its website. To access these you must join their free website.

You Can... Get support from government agencies

Environmental sustainability is a whole-school agenda and should be considered at all levels of school life. It is an aspect of modern education that deserves serious support from the top down. As a reflection of this, the two learning departments that arguably have the most impact on schools, The Department for Children, Schools and Families (DCSF) and the National College for School Leadership (NCSL), have both launched environmental programmes. These are aimed at working with school leadership and communities in order to promote environmental sustainability.

Thinking points

● Educational research in environmental sustainability is limited. However, what research has shown is that, because the area is new, sustainable schools naturally allow opportunities for experimental models of leadership such as shared or distributive leadership. These professional development models can provide opportunities for the leaders of tomorrow to lead in their school today.

● Schools with strong moral values will find a natural place for environmental sustainability in their school vision and school aims. In all likelihood your aims will, if they do not reflect sustainability, need little changing to do so. Note that changing the wording of your school's aims requires the consultation of the governors as well as staff to ensure that all agree on the wording – after all these aims are what your school stands for.

Tips, ideas and activities

● For more information on leadership in sustainable schools search the NCSL website (www.ncsl.org.uk) for 'leading sustainable schools'

● All agencies agree that addressing sustainability in schools not only offers a valuable environmental lesson but makes good financial sense. It is also an important area that genuinely unites the curriculum with *Every Child Matters*.

● For the first time in 2006/07, the Teaching Awards programme included an award for sustainable development. Your school could be eligible for an award.

● The DCSF has developed a comprehensive strategy for sustainable schools called Sustainable Schools for Pupils, Communities and the Environment. It is available as a download from: http://publications.teachernet.gov.uk; search under 'Sustainable Schools for pupils'.

● Schools can work towards a sustainable Kitemark from the DCSF. The information for this can be accessed on their dedicated website (http://www.sustainablelearning.info). It is worth noting that the evidence needed for this accreditation can also be shared with other sustainable awards such as Eco-Schools.

● The NCSL has awarded £5000 grants to over 50 schools to act as lead schools for sustainability. Their remit is to:
  ● write a case study that describes their leadership of a sustainable school
  ● promote the leadership of sustainability with other local schools
  ● build a local, sustainable school leadership network.
For more information go to www.ncsl.org.uk.

You Can... Gain financial support through Solar4Schools

At the end of 2006 the Department for Trade and Industry (DTI) launched a £50 million scheme designed to reduce the cost of renewable energy equipment by part-funding sustainable energy installations on public and private sector buildings. The Low Carbon Emissions Programme (LCEP) is specifically designed for sites such as schools, and grants are awarded by the DTI to cover half the cost of solar panels. Solar4Schools has established links with a number of premier energy suppliers in order to support schools with their bids.

Thinking points

● We live in a cloudy country and, as such, it would be reasonable to assume that solar energy is not the energy source for us. However, energy-producing solar cells (Photovoltaic solar cells, or PV cells) do not require direct sunlight as they work on absorbing photons. Consequently, they work as well in the UK as they would in any sunny country.

● If we were to cover the roof space of all state buildings – schools, hospitals, colleges – with PV solar cells they would create enough energy to support all public buildings. If we covered every roof space with PV cells we would vastly outstrip the amount of energy created by fossil fuels and other energy sources.

● Portugal is leading Europe with its solar energy plants. The Serpa solar power project covers an area of 150 acres and produces enough energy for 8000 homes.

Tips, ideas and activities

● When considering solar panelling do some background research. If your building is in a conservation zone then you will need to be careful where you site your panels. Also, survey your roof. It will need to be structurally strong as solar panels are heavy.

● A single 4 kilowatt PV solar array currently costs £20,000 before the 50% DTI grant. Even at £10,000 school leaders are obliged to have this agreed by the governing body. It is important that the people with financial authority in your school – your headteacher and chair of governors – are on-board with the project from the very start. It is a considerable amount of money that must be accounted for.

● Be reasonable about your solar expectation and equally ensure that those around you are just as aware of what to expect. The solar panels will not replace your current energy costs though they will contribute towards off-setting them.

● Schools that support solar energy are demonstrating to the school community that there is a reasonable alternative to the current energy forms.

● Solar Aid is Solar4Schools' sister charity. This charity works in sub-Saharan Africa and provides solar support to communities with poor energy supplies. Solar Aid is working towards developing solar radios, mobile phones, laptops, lighting and other everyday devices to help support these people. Ask your class what energy devices they use at home. Could they survive with no energy? In the modern world, it is arguable that energy is as important as medication, food and clean water.

● If you are considering solar panelling these sites may help:
www.solar4schools.co.uk
www.solar-aid.org

You Can... **Apply for Eco-Schools awards**

Eco-Schools is an international award programme run by the Foundation for Environmental Education (FEE) in over 40 countries and 40,000 schools worldwide. Its core message is to guide schools on their sustainable journey by providing a framework to help embed sustainable principles into the heart of school life. Schools can apply for three awards – Bronze, Silver and Green Flag – that are internationally recognised as having achieved a standard of sustainable learning in school.

Thinking points

● The key questions that schools should be asking themselves when applying for Eco-School awards are: Why is this important? What is the big picture? Who is this going to benefit? Are we in control of our school's site and environment, and if not how can we begin to make a difference? With this in mind, Eco-Schools was set up to support schools that are willing to work towards improving their environment by taking those small steps that can make a big difference.

● The environmental message is not new. Schools have been teaching children about this for many years. The difference is that we are undergoing significant climate change around the world and it is having a direct impact on all our lives. It is no longer theoretical. It is now an imperative to get everybody on-board and involved. This message is for our children's future. And ours.

Tips, ideas and activities

● Begin by identifying an action team ideally made up of children, a governor, a member of staff and a senior school leader. This will allow the group leader to delegate tasks but, importantly, it will also support the spread of the environmental message.

● Perform an environmental review. This will give you your baseline assessment, which in turn will direct your initial plans of action. A comprehensive environmental review can be downloaded from the Eco-Schools website (www.eco-schools. org.uk). Alternatively, a slimmed down review is available on pages 59–61.

● Identify your plans of action. Keep your steps small and manageable. Common sense says it is far better to complete one project than start many and not see them through. A proforma action plan grid is available on the Eco-Schools website, however you may wish to use your standard school action plan for school continuity.

● Ideally link your projects and plans to the school curriculum and *Every Child Matters*. See page 11 for ideas.

● Eco-Schools focus on nine areas: water, biodiversity, energy, global perspective, healthy living, litter, school grounds, transport, waste. Link your projects to one of these areas.

● When you have completed an audit, identified a project, written your plan and begun development you may want to see if you are eligible for an award. Both Bronze and Silver awards are given through online self-assessment. The Green Flag award is in recognition of outstanding contribution towards environmental learning and will, as a result, require rigorous and robust evidence to qualify. The Green Flag is a schools' version of the Blue Flag seen on beaches with outstanding environmental standards.

Environmental action plan

School name:

Subject leader:

Academic year:

Every Child Matters outcomes:
- Being Healthy
- Staying Safe
- Enjoying & Achieving
- Making a Positive Contribution
- Achieving Economic Well-being

Links to school aims/vision:

Environmental focus:

Actions required (steps to be taken)	Action by whom	Action by when	Funding	Monitoring – how and who	Notes on progress

Environmental review
Energy

Is there someone in your school who has special responsibility for monitoring the consumption of energy (electricity, heating, etc.) in the school? If there is, who is it?	☐ Yes ☐ No _____
Are the energy meters (e.g. electricity meters) easily visible to pupils? Are pupils involved in taking and displaying readings?	☐ Yes ☐ No ☐ Yes ☐ No
Do the school windows have double glazing, triple glazing or energy-saving glass? If yes, in how many rooms? (If all, write 'all'.)	☐ Yes ☐ No _____
Are any external (outside) doors self-closing? If yes, how many doors are self-closing? (If all, write 'all'.)	☐ Yes ☐ No _____
Are any internal (inside) doors self-closing? If yes, how many doors are self-closing? (If all, write 'all'.)	☐ Yes ☐ No _____
Are low-energy light bulbs used in school?	☐ Yes ☐ No
Does each classroom have its own heating thermostat? If no, how many rooms have a thermostat? (If none, write 'none'.)	☐ Yes ☐ No _____
Are lights and electrical items turned off when not in use?	☐ Yes ☐ No ☐ Sometimes

Does the school have any of the following sources of renewable energy?
☐ Wind generator   ☐ Solar water PV heating panels
☐ Wood fuel boiler   ☐ Ground source heat pump

Litter

How serious is the problem of rubbish/litter in the school grounds? ☐ Very serious ☐ Not too bad ☐ More or less litter-free	
Does your school have a clear anti-litter policy?	☐ Yes ☐ No
Are there any areas inside the school buildings that are littered where there are no bins?	☐ Yes ☐ No
Are there any areas in the school grounds that are littered where there are no bins?	☐ Yes ☐ No

Waste minimization/recycling

Does the school carefully control the use of resources such as paper, pencils, ink cartridges, pens, envelopes, etc?

☐ No, there seems to be little control.   ☐ Yes, but control is not very tight.

☐ Yes, control of these materials is very strict.

Does the school buy stationery products (paper, pencils, pens, etc.) made from recycled content?

☐ Yes (where possible)   ☐ No   ☐ Sometimes

Are hand towels and other disposable paper products purchased with recycled content? If some, note which products are and which aren't.	☐ Yes ☐ Some ☐ No _____

Does the school recycle any of the following items of school waste?

☐ Paper   ☐ Cardboard   ☐ Plastic

☐ Inkjet cartridges   ☐ Vending machine cups   ☐ Other

Please describe other materials recycled. _____

Do you run any other recycling schemes to raise money for the school and/or involve the local community, e.g. mobile phones, jumble sales?	☐ Yes ☐ No
Does the school encourage reuse of materials, e.g. water bottles?	☐ Yes ☐ No
Does the school have any policies to reduce waste?	☐ Yes ☐ No

Water

Is there a water meter to record water use in school?	☐ Yes ☐ No
Is the meter easily visible to pupils?	☐ Yes ☐ No
Are pupils involved in taking readings?	☐ Yes ☐ No
Are the toilets designed to reduce water loss e.g. low-volume flush, flush-on-demand urinals, etc? If yes, how many of the toilets are fitted with such devices? (list, or state 'all'.)	☐ Yes ☐ No _____
Are hand-basin taps of the push-on or self-stopping type? If yes, how many? (list, or state 'all'.)	☐ Yes ☐ No _____

Are taps left running?

☐ Always   ☐ Sometimes   ☐ Never

Approximately how long do leaks take to repair?

☐ 2–3 days   ☐ 4–7 days   ☐ More than 7 days

How often does the school run water-saving campaigns?

☐ Regularly   ☐ Occasionally   ☐ Never

Transport

Do you monitor how pupils travel to school?	☐ Yes	☐ No

If yes, how many pupils use the following transport to or from school – note total count of pupils
☐ Walk   ☐ Bus   ☐ Cycle ☐ Share a taxi   ☐ Share a car   ☐ Travel as a single passenger in car Has this data been mapped?   ☐ Yes   ☐ No

Does the school have dry and secure cycle storage?	☐ Yes	☐ No
If yes, is there sufficient space for all users?	☐ Yes	☐ No

Does the school offer cycle instruction?	☐ Yes	☐ No
If yes, does it include on-road training?	☐ Yes	☐ No
If yes, does it meet the national standard?	☐ Yes	☐ No

Does the school have a network of 'safe routes' to walk or cycle?	☐ Yes	☐ No

Does the school have any of the following:		
Walking bus scheme	☐ Yes	☐ No
Cycle train	☐ Yes	☐ No
Park and stride	☐ Yes	☐ No
Other similar scheme	☐ Yes	☐ No

Does the school organise regular 'walk to school' or 'cycle to school' events?	☐ Yes	☐ No
Do any of the school transport vehicles (buses, taxis, etc.) run on alternative fuels such as electricity, land-fill gas or vegetable-derived oils?	☐ Yes	☐ No
Does the school have a school travel plan?	☐ Yes	☐ No
Does the school have a pedestrian and cycle entrance that is separate from vehicle access?	☐ Yes	☐ No

Biodiversity

Do the school grounds staff use chemical pesticides and herbicides? ☐ Often   ☐ Occasionally   ☐ Never

Does the school have any plants in containers, pots or beds in the school grounds?	☐ Yes, lots ☐ Yes, some ☐ No
Does the school have a wildlife, or conservation area?	☐ Yes ☐ No
Does the school have links with any local or national environmental organisations, e.g. the Woodland Trust? If yes, with whom? (list)	☐ Yes ☐ No _____

School travel survey

Date: _____ School: _____ Class: _____

To be completed by the whole class, by a show of hands.
Please write TOTAL NUMBER of hands shown in each box.

1   Number of pupils present _____ absent _____

2   How do pupils usually get to school (for the main part of their journey)?

walk	bus	train	cycle
car	school bus	tube	other

3   How would they like to get to school?

walk	bus	train	cycle
car	school bus	tube	other

4   For those pupils who travel by car, do they car share*? Yes No
(*Car share means that they go by car with people who go to the school but
are not in their family.)

5a   For those pupils who travel by car, where does the person driving the car go
after they have dropped them off at school?

home	work	another school	other

5b   If the person driving the car goes to another school after they drop them off,
where do they go after that?

home	work	other

6   How do pupils usually go home from school (for the main part of their journey)?

walk	bus	train	cycle
car	school bus	tube	other

Thank you for **completing** the survey.

Index

■SCHOLASTIC

Also available in this series:

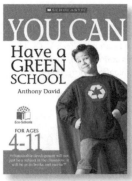

ISBN 978-1407-10083-8

ISBN 978-1407-10070-8

ISBN 978-0439-94534-9

ISBN 978-0439-94535-6

ISBN 978-0439-96522-4

ISBN 978-0439-96523-1

ISBN 978-0439-96534-7

ISBN 978-0439-96539-2

ISBN 978-0439-96540-8

ISBN 978-0439-96554-5

ISBN 978-0439-96555-2

ISBN 978-0439-94530-1

ISBN 978-0439-94531-8

ISBN 978-0439-94559-2

ISBN 978-0439-94554-7

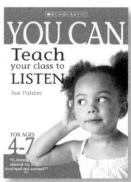

ISBN 978-0439-94532-5

ISBN 978-0439-94533-2

To find out more, call: 0845 603 9091
or visit our website www.scholastic.co.uk